MORE PRAISE FOR SINGLETASKING

"Zack's system is thoughtful, simple, and practical, so it's no surprise that it works."
  —Richard J. McAlonan, Executive Director, Ernst & Young LLP

"Zack makes a compelling case for the merits of living a singletasked life."
  —Rachel Lam, Senior Vice President and Group Managing Director
  Time Warner Investments

"Multitasking is madness—you wouldn't want to be operated on by a surgeon who was checking her email every five minutes, would you? Devora offers simple, straightforward advice for getting far more done than you ever would hopping around like a frog on a hot skillet."
  —Deborah S. Cohn, former Trademarks Commissioner
  United States Patent and Trademark Office

"In our hyperconnected world where we fear missing out on anything, Zack delivers a message we need to hear—the key to personal and organizational success is focusing on what matters most."
  —Patrick Fitzgerald, Vice President, SiriusXM Radio

"Zack provides the artillery to slay the multitasking monster, creating wholeness, happiness, and peak performance."
  —Amy Lemon, Program Manager, Smithsonian Institution

"Zack gives us a much-needed wake-up call about the dangers of a distracted mind."
  —Jeff Weirens, M&A Consulting Leader, Deloitte Consulting LLP

"A great read while you're catching up on email, finishing that proposal, and preparing performance feedback for your staff . . . Zack connects with her readers in a light, funny style that makes this book a delightful read."
  —Mike Brennan, retired intelligence executive, National Reconnaissance Office

"This book could save your life. Multitasking has become a fatal distraction that can ruin your health, your relationships, and your work. But now there's a cure: singletasking. Read this intensely engaging, laugh-out-loud funny, and down-to-earth practical book now—you'll be glad you did, and so will those you live and work with."
  —Jim Kouzes, coauthor of *The Leadership Challenge* and
  Dean's Executive Fellow of Leadership, Leavey School of Business,
  Santa Clara University

"Don't be seduced by the false promise of multitasking! Instead, be seduced by the insight and humor of Devora Zack, who shows you how to really make your mind work at peak efficiency."

—**Shai Novik, President, OPKO Biologics**

"Multitasking is like trying to look in two directions at once: it seems like it'd be cool, but it can't be done and makes your head hurt trying. Devora Zack helps you accomplish more than you ever thought possible using tips and techniques that genuinely work!"

—**David Meisegeier, Vice President, ICF International**

"I used to multitask constantly, thinking it was the only way to get through my day. After reading this book, I'm a convert."

—**Hiro Yamaguchi, General Manager of Corporate Strategy, TEPCO, Japan**

"Zack dispels our basic assumptions that multitasking is a sine qua non to achievement and proves in a most informative and entertaining manner that focused singletasking is the true path to achieving our goals."

—**Howard Wiener, Partner, KPMG LLP**

"Management myth buster Devora Zack's new target is the fabled beast known as multitasking. While a one-man band may entertain and amuse, Zack's new book repeatedly proves that the dedicated, single-task-focused individual achieves quantifiable results time and time again."

—**Dave Summers, Director of Digital Media Production,**
  New Media Stage Management, American Management Association

"When confronted with multiple tasks that must be completed expeditiously, it's easy to fall into the trap of believing that they all can be tackled simultaneously. Zack demonstrates (with evidence) why we've had it all wrong."

—**Ann-Marie Luciano, Partner, Dickstein Shapiro LLP**

"As a customer of Devora's services at two Fortune 500 companies, I can attest that her methods produce tangible results. Singletasking identifies opportunities for improvement and targets the right actions to bring out the best in people and organizations."

—**Jeff Martin, former human resources executive, CSC and America Online**

"I always suspected that those who prided themselves on being able to do a lot of things simultaneously weren't necessarily superior; this book proves it."

—**P. J. Kuyper, President and CEO, Motion Picture Licensing Corporation**

"I thought I was supposed to pride myself on being able to do a lot of things simultaneously—but I'm too exhausted! Thanks to Devora Zack for showing us a better way."

—**Peter Borden, Vice President, Client Services, SapientNitro**

SINGLETASKING

Other books by Devora Zack:

Managing for People Who Hate Managing:
Be a Success by Being Yourself

Networking for People Who Hate Networking:
A Field Guide for Introverts, the Overwhemed,
and the Underconnected

SINGLETASKING

Get More Done—
*   One Thing at a Time*

DEVORA ZACK

Berrett–Koehler Publishers, Inc.
a BK Life book

Berrett-Koehler Publishers, Inc.
1333 Broadway, Suite 1000
Oakland, CA 94612-1921
Tel: (510) 817-2277   Fax: (510) 817-2278
www.bkconnection.com

Ordering Information

Quantity sales. Special discounts are available on quantity purchases by corporations, associations, and others. For details, contact the "Special Sales Department" at the Berrett-Koehler address above.

Individual sales. Berrett-Koehler publications are available through most bookstores. They can also be ordered directly from Berrett-Koehler: Tel: (800) 929-2929; Fax: (802) 864-7626; www.bkconnection.com

Orders for college textbook/course adoption use. Please contact Berrett-Koehler: Tel: (800) 929-2929; Fax: (802) 864-7626.

Orders by U.S. trade bookstores and wholesalers. Please contact Ingram Publisher Services, Tel: (800) 509-4887; Fax: (800) 838-1149; E-mail: customer.service@ingrampublisherservices.com; or visit www.ingrampublisherservices.com/Ordering for details about electronic ordering.

Berrett-Koehler and the BK logo are registered trademarks of Berrett-Koehler Publishers, Inc.

Printed in the United States of America

Berrett-Koehler books are printed on long-lasting acid-free paper. When it is available, we choose paper that has been manufactured by environmentally responsible processes. These may include using trees grown in sustainable forests, incorporating recycled paper, minimizing chlorine in bleaching, or recycling the energy produced at the paper mill.

Library of Congress Cataloging-in-Publication Data
Zack, Devora.
Singletasking : get more done—one thing at a time / Devora Zack. —First edition.
     pages cm
Includes bibliographical references.
     ISBN 978-1-62656-261-5 (pbk.)
     1. Time management. 2. Human multitasking. I. Title.
HD69.T54Z33 2015
650.1'1—dc23
                                                      2015000854

First Edition

20 19 18 17 16 15   10 9 8 7 6 5 4 3 2 1

Text design and composition: Seventeenth Street Studios
Cover design: Dan Tesser/Studio Carnelian
Copyeditor: Todd Manza
Proofreader: Laurie Dunne
Indexer: Richard Evans

To my dearest reader:

You are hereby released from
the temptation to overachieve.

Your friend:
Devora Zack

P.S. You're welcome.

Carpe diem.

For my sons . . .

who charmingly prove the merits of singletasking,
even under the most rigorous trials.

CONTENTS

PREFACE

MYTH

My life demands that I do several things at once.

REALITY

I must be fully present as I travel through my days.

The successful man is the average man, focused.

ANONYMOUS

Why Me?

I am despondent over my ample qualifications to write this book.

That I wrote it verifies my good will and poor judgment. Why would I voluntarily take on the task of authoring a book when more pressing matters demand my immediate attention?

Let's breeze through one of my basic weekday mornings. By 8:30 I've exercised, done a little writing at my neighborhood café, scanned the headlines, reorganized my to-do list, whizzed to the local grocery, woken and fed my three glorious (aka "grumpy-it's-a-school-day-again") sons, prepped lunches, run the dishwasher, imperceptibly tidied up, tossed in a laundry load, completed three round-trip school runs, returned several client messages, and am en route to my first meeting of the day—chagrined that the clock is closing in on 9:00.

Don't be impressed. I'm typically burned out by 11:30.

Upon arrival at my office, I'm not congratulating myself on my efficiency. No. Awaiting me is a lovely array of supremely urgent messages, meetings, interviews, conference calls, a lunchtime presentation, and a manuscript deadline. How will I ever catch up?

I won't! I am a failure. I may as well collapse facedown on my keyboard right now.

Nothing can save me, with the exception of . . . singletasking!

Me and You

Forget about my career as an author, speaker, and consultant. What matters more is that I understand on a visceral level the titanic demands facing my readers daily—and I have a solution that truly works.

Nothing is more annoying than getting advice from so-called experts completely out of touch with the reality of normal lives:

- "Delegate 90 percent of your tasks; free yourself for creative strategic planning."
- "Reduce your workload to fifteen minutes a day; only do the real essentials!"
- "Don't take on any more responsibilities until your schedule opens up."
- "Take several vacations a year to rejuvenate."

Has your head blown up?

Do not despair. I am not one of those types of experts. Their misguided advice is decidedly not the solution to your travails. I've got the cure, and I'm calling it *singletasking*.

Successful singletasking means managing your own sweet self (starting with your thoughts) and your encompassing environment (including your relationships).

Bliss is a slim volume away. The remedy has arrived, in the helpful form of a fast, fun read. Did I mention practical?

I am confident the two of us can muddle through the murk and emerge brighter, happier, and more efficacious by the far end of this book's cover.

INTRODUCTION

MYTH

Multitasking leads to success.

REALITY

Multitasking leads to mistakes.

You would not believe how difficult it is
to be simple and clear. People are afraid that
they may be seen as a simpleton. In reality,
just the opposite is true.

JACK WELCH

Evelyn was excited about an essay she had written for a class she was taking. She asked if she could read it to me.

"Sure! I'd love to hear it!" Then I glanced down at my iPhone. Big mistake.

I assumed she'd need a moment to retrieve her essay, and I had been waiting all day to hear the results of a recently submitted project proposal. There was an email from the prospect.

Evelyn began to read, but by now I was far away.

"Wait!" I said. Evelyn stopped.

My glance at the email had revealed that my company's proposal was not selected for the contract on which I had spent the better part of a week. "Oh no!" I wailed. "That is ridiculous! They totally blew it!"

By now Evelyn couldn't hide her annoyance. "Never mind."

I begged forgiveness, tossed my iPhone facedown on the table, and convinced her to start reading her essay to me all over again.

From this, I realized two basic facts:

1. I couldn't be a truly present listener with my attention split between Evelyn's essay and the disappointing news I had to share tomorrow with my colleagues.
2. When visiting with a friend in the evening, it is absolutely unnecessary to check on the results of a work proposal.

Let's Get It Started

Do you ever look at the clock upon the day's end and wonder where the time went? Are you nonstop busy yet lack a sense of accomplishment? Does your to-do list grow rather than shrink, despite your best efforts?

Please say it's not just me.

In my research for a book about singletasking, I spoke with hundreds of people. The majority reacted along the lines of "I need that!" Or alternatively, "My coworker/spouse/friend/boss/employee needs that!" Yet the idea of relinquishing multitasking turns out to be surprisingly controversial. The intensity of responses reminded me of how certain folks get revved up over politics or religion. Some people were incensed, refusing to accept that singletasking is remotely plausible. Multitasking is an ingrained cultural expectation, woven into the fabric of our times.

Consider the following response to my suggestion that a credible and superior alternative to multitasking exists: "I like the idea of singletasking but I'm afraid it's not for me. Frankly, singletasking sounds like a luxury, and not one that people in business can generally afford. Does it sound nice to focus on one thing at a time? Sure! Would I have time to sleep? I'm doubtful. Please prove me wrong!"

Got it. I will. I like a challenge.

Singletasking is not a luxury; it is a necessity. You can accomplish far more doing one thing at a time, plus enjoy sleep. In fact, increased restorative time is both an outcome of—and a contributor to—a singletasked life.

My work is further fueled by comments such as, "I multi-task all the time. I have to. I wouldn't be able to get anything done otherwise. It is impossible to function without it."

Offering an alternative to the societal norm has never been easy. Galileo lived in an era when the Earth was widely considered to be the center of the universe. He challenged this belief, boldly attesting that the planets—Earth included—rotate around the sun. He was consequently investigated by the Roman Inquisition, found guilty of heresy, and placed under house arrest. Yikes.

That multitasking has a real following is quite the understatement. When I say it is an illusion—well, let's face it, that's consultant heresy. I'll never work in this town again!

When mavericks go against the grain, two components have to be in place. First, we have to really, really believe in what we espouse. Second, we cannot stop ourselves from sharing what we know to be true.

And so, my friends, I present to you the Singletasking Principle:

▶ **Get more done, one thing at a time.**

Recall a time you were counting something—money, items, your pulse, or accolades—lost your train of thought, and had to start again. There are two likely reasons you lost count. One is internal: your mind wandered. The second is that an external stimulus distracted you.

The former demonstrates how an unruly mind can derail even a simple task. The latter shows how succumbing to external distractions wastes, rather than saves, time. Either way, an interruption scrambled your focus, decreasing your productivity. You'll now need to start all over on your singularly important job of counting.

This book provides a system with versatile tools to help you restore your attention to what matters most. You will learn how to manage your mind, your environment, and all those pesky people who come between you and your potential. You will gain insights that enable you to consistently finish what you begin. By immersing yourself in one task at a time, one moment at a time, you'll accomplish more while enjoying deeper, stronger relationships.

What about distractions? You'll learn how to mitigate disruptions originating in your mind as well as those meandering around your workplace.

Go ahead; let free a sigh of relief.

Welcome to Singletasking

The themes of this book are presented in three primary sections:

Part 1: Reclaim Your Life

Part 2: Regain Control

Part 3: Recall What Matters

Part 1 provides the groundwork. This section debunks multitasking as a viable solution to a hectic life, introduces singletasking as the antidote to our frenetic world, provides a self-assessment to determine your current approach to tasks, and explains how we got into this predicament.

Part 2 offers techniques on how to guide our thoughts, workplace, and relationships. Here we deep dive into applying the singletasking definition provided in the preface—managing yourself and your environment.

Part 3 teaches you how to rejuvenate, improve home life, and live in a calmer, happier way. This section expands the Singletasking Principle beyond the workplace.

Each component influences the others. When you refine your thought process, your relationships are positively impacted. When you take control of your environment, the day flows more smoothly. And so on. Therefore, key elements are interwoven throughout the sections.

It Can't Be Real . . . Can It?

Perhaps singletasking seems a tad unrealistic. Such a concept may appear charming, yet you have more on your plate than I could possibly imagine!

Except that I'm also living that kind of life, and all the methods in this book have been created and tested by real people and really work.

When I tell you that multitasking absolutely backfires, this is not some crackerjack opinion that I've conjured. The assertions in this book are backed up by a combination of neuroscience, globally conducted research, and cross-disciplinary studies.

Here's an amuse-bouche: switching focus lowers productivity while increasing the number of hours required to complete tasks. Researchers at Harvard University found that the most productive employees change focus relatively few times, whereas frenetic workers switch focus up to five hundred times a day.

In short, habitually switching between tasks correlates with poor productivity.[1]

Additionally, multitaskers are more susceptible than single-taskers to interference (sacrificing performance on a primary task to let in other sources of information), less effective at suppressing activation of irrelevant tasks, and slower to focus. What researchers have dubbed "heavy media multitasking" correlates with high susceptibility to distraction and a poor ability to filter stimuli.

Just Do It!

Joining the ranks of the highly productive and efficient does not require a societal shift or a global reconfiguration. You can make a change all on your own. Simply practice the accessible techniques offered here and you will learn how to consistently direct your attention to one task at a time.

I understand that temptations run high to surrender to multitasking. I have one teeny question: How's it working for you so far? And some follow-up questions, Your Honor: Does being distracted, unfocused, and scattered make you more productive, calm, and relaxed? How do you like it when other people interrupt, seem to half-listen, or ask you to repeat what you just said? And do you check messages when in meetings, read emails when on the phone, or lack discipline when you need to concentrate?

This book will teach you to be more productive, immerse yourself in tasks, and reduce distractions. This is a book that teaches you—reminds you—how to be here, now; how to live in a state of creative flow; how to stop the madness.

Singletasking will change the quality of your life. Take the plunge. Commit!

You can do it.

PART ONE

Reclaim Your Life

Things which matter most
must never be at the expense of
things which matter least.

JOHANN WOLFGANG
VON GOETHE

The Multitasking Myth

1

MYTH

I'm great at multitasking.

REALITY

Multitasking is neurologically impossible.

No man is free
who is not master of himself.

EPICTETUS

Multitasking fails us.

Let me take that one step further. Multitasking doesn't even exist. We'll circle back to this alarming yet scientifically backed claim later.

Why are so many people drawn into the albatross of multitasking? We are collectively thwarted by modern-day plagues such as:

- Too much to do, too little time
- Cluttered life, cluttered mind
- Growing piles of daily demands
- A whirlwind of distractions

Nooo! [Cue eerie Halloween music.]

This list is the tip of the iceberg. Go ahead; brainstorm a few dozen examples of your own. I'll wait here, tapping my foot, growing ever more anxious that I'm wasting my irreplaceable time.

When you return, check out how one guy I interviewed described multitasking in daily life: "What is the impact of multitasking when looking at text messages while driving? Reading the newspaper while talking on the phone to colleagues? Watching *NFL Live* when your wife wants to talk about schedules? You run into the car ahead of you, agree to finish a project before it can possibly be done, and schedule a business trip on your father-in-law's birthday."

In a fruitless effort to compensate for the tsunami we call our lives, we try to tackle several tasks at once . . . making distracted living rampant. We lose concentration, heighten stress, and senselessly fret over items unrelated to the task at hand. We are relentlessly disrespectful to the people right in front of us—colleagues, customers, vendors, employees, cohorts, and our own family.

Fragmented attention (aka multitasking) fractures results and foils relationships.

A Monster in Our Midst

What makes multitasking so enticing?

We know of the dangers of texting and driving, yet many of us still do it. How can we circumvent distraction? Why is it so difficult to immerse ourselves in a single task at a time? Because lurking around every turn is what I call the multitask monster. Many are thwarted by this compelling creature.

One of his primary tricks is pulling our attention toward unrelated obligations as we work. He looms over our desks, lumbering around our workplace, two heads recklessly swinging in opposite directions, daring us to focus on one over the other. As we stare in despair at our stealthily expanding in-box, the multitask monster soothingly whispers into our ears the Sole Solution: "Tackle two, three, four at once! It is your *only hope.*"

Worse, seemingly everyone else has taken on the multitask monster as a revered guide, responding to his every beck and call.

Resist! Stop the madness! Gather your resilience and kick that multitask monster out the door. Multitask monsters are like ocean sirens luring sailors to disaster—though notably less well groomed.

What if I asked you to banish the multitask monster for one day? Could you do it? What would stop you? Can you give it a go? What results will you reap?

One client reflected, "I've always prided myself on being a multitasker over the years, but if I were to do honest self-evaluation today, I realize there are pitfalls to all this madness!"

Another acknowledged, "When I do more than one thing at a time I never do anything particularly well."

The hard fact is that attempting to multitask correlates with low productivity.[1] By definition, doing more than one thing at a time means you are distracted. The only way to do anything particularly well—or, let's raise the bar, *spectacularly* well—is through full task engagement. As I heard a father sagely explain to his son, a newly minted college grad, "At any given time, you can do one thing well or two things poorly."

The Allure of Distraction

We are distracted. This does not serve us well.

Don't blame yourself entirely. Cultural expectations—based on technological advances—have resulted in unrealistic demands. We are expected to absorb a torrent of information from a plethora of media without pause. We are to be constantly accessible.

Many of us react to the alarming pile of demands by splitting our focus among tasks. We are in the midst of an increasing trend toward what Linda Stone calls "continuous partial attention"—giving superficial, simultaneous attention to competing streams of information.[2] Living in our own personal big bang, we feel unable to keep pace with the frenetically expanding universe encircling our lives. Again and again I hear, "The more I try to keep up, the more overwhelmed I become."

A slew of people suffer from the misconception that multitasking is necessary to cope with task overload. This always backfires.

Multitasking is misleading. Rather than mitigating demands, it magnifies our problems. Our brains are incapable of honing in on more than one item at a time.

Multitasking blocks the flow of information into short-term memory. Data that doesn't make it into short-term memory cannot be transferred into long-term memory for recall. Therefore, multitasking lowers our ability to accomplish tasks.

We are losing our ability to focus. We are scattered. We are impolite. We cause—and suffer from—accidents. We are unproductive. We relinquish control. We pretend to multitask.

Why did I say "pretend"? Because multitasking doesn't exist! I'll keep sneaking in this factoid until you're ready to hear it. It's make-believe! Think Zeus throwing lightning bolts. Or Casper the Friendly Ghost.

Everybody Loves a Neuroscientist

As any neighborhood neuroscientist will attest, the brain can only focus on one thing at a time.

Allow me to expand. The brain is incapable of simultaneously processing separate streams of information from attention-demanding tasks. What we conversationally reference as multi-tasking is technically called task-switching—moving rapidly and ineffectively among tasks.

As Dr. Eyal Ophir, a neuroscientist at Stanford University, explains, "Humans don't really multitask, we task-switch . . . switch[ing] very quickly between tasks." Although this feels like multitasking, the brain is incapable of focusing on two things at once. Plus, performance suffers as attention shifts back and forth.[3]

Not only that, get a load of this from Dr. Earl Miller at the Massachusetts Institute of Technology: "You cannot focus on one [task] while doing [an]other. That's because of what's called interference between the two tasks. . . . People can't multitask very well, and when people say they can, they're deluding themselves. The brain is very good at deluding itself."[4]

To recap, actual multitasking is not possible, and what is commonly labeled as multitasking is really task-switching. We task-switch within tenths of a second; we don't consciously notice delays. So from here forward I will alternatively reference multitasking as task-switching, "attempts to multitask," or "so-called multitasking." Occasionally I'll just say multitasking, although you and I both know that is just shorthand. Most defenders of multitasking do not have a grasp of its actual meaning. I don't intend this as a slam. Multitaskers are only halfway paying attention to what I'm saying anyway.

Even electrical synapses short-circuit over so-called multitasking. As one client shared with me, "I met up with my boss as I walked in this morning. He was talking to me as I entered my PIN into the door lock. I said to him, 'I can't multitask,' meaning I couldn't listen to him and enter my number at the same time. He told me multitasking also backfires in the context of electrical engineering, the way circuits are designed. If you try to make a circuit do more than one thing, its efficiency is reduced."

My client's boss has a doctorate in electrical engineering. In fact, according to the Oxford English Dictionary, the word *multitasking* is derived from computer processing, emerging in the English lexicon at the time of the first computer.

> **Multitasking:** [noun] 1. Computing simultaneous execution of more than one program or task by a single computer processor. 2. Handling of more than one task at the same time by a single person.

Replacing rapid-fire shifts with attention on one task at a time enables us to achieve more in less time. We wind up ahead.

When Multitasking Isn't Multitasking

Some folks angrily retort, "I can hold a conversation and empty the dishwasher. I can listen to the radio and drive! That's multitasking."

Allow me to begin by saying that I admire your feisty spirit. That said, Dr. David Meyer can clear things up: "Under most conditions, the brain simply cannot do two complex tasks at the same time. It can happen only when the two tasks ... don't compete with each other for the same mental resources."[5]

Multitasking means combining two or more activities, potentially causing at least one to receive inadequate attention. Activities that require virtually no conscious effort can be performed in conjunction with primary tasks and do not fall in the bandwidth of multitasking. "Simple" tasks are automated, low-level functions, including rote activities that do not require concentration.

Engaging in two unrelated tasks at the same time when at least one does not demand conscious effort is not multitasking. Activities in this category vary based on one's experience and surroundings. For example, driving to the local grocery store is a basic, mundane event for many, yet a new driver must give her full attention to the same event. Doing dishes takes no conscious effort, unless this is an atypical chore for you. Most of us can drive and chat with a passenger or listen to the news and tidy up.

Although autopilot tasks vary based on background and intention, activities that may fall into this category include:

- Listening to music
- Filing papers
- Basic food preparation
- Simple repair or craftwork

It's a slippery slope. Unexpected distraction could cause a favorite passage to be missed, a document to be misplaced, a meal to burn, or glue to spill. We can be driving along a familiar route, space out, and miss a usual exit. The actual cause is a brain that temporarily disengages from our actions. The unruly mind spaces out, goes somewhere else entirely, and fails to synchronize with the current mission. It was multitasking.

There is a fine line between engaging in a largely reflexive activity and maintaining awareness of an unexpected twist. Perhaps you can drive to work without thinking ninety-nine percent of the time. But if a car unexpectedly swerves into your lane, are your reflexes ready to react?

Another danger is confusing automated and attention-demanding tasks. For example, people mistakenly believe they can text and walk, remaining fully aware of their surroundings. We will soon discover the fallacy of this belief.

Although there are instances when engaging in two *noncompeting* activities can be beneficial, choose carefully. Squeezing a stress ball while on a conference call can be a positive release, whereas checking email is a distraction. Stretching while watching a television show is far more beneficial than just sitting on the couch. Listening to upbeat music while exercising can heighten the effectiveness of a workout, although conversing or reading while on a treadmill typically reduces calories burned. Engaging in two noncompeting activities when at least one is automatic is generally harmless; pursuing competing tasks can exact a very high toll.

The Price We Pay

Raise your hand if you have observed people doing any of the following:

- Colliding with others while looking at a phone
- Not driving when the light turns green
- Playing games on handheld devices at professional events
- Not noticing when arriving at the front of a line at a shop or café

These minor irritations are the tip of the iceberg.

Multitasking takes a terrible toll.

In the United States, distracted driving kills tens of thousands of people each year, with an economic toll from injury and loss of life amounting to $871 billion annually. Distracted driving and driving under the influence (DUI) are nearly tied as the top two causes of deadly car crashes. DUI accounts for 18 percent of deaths in motor vehicle crashes, with distracted driving a factor in at least 17 percent of fatal vehicular accidents. The true percentage is likely much higher. Distracted driving is under-reported, because police have difficulty identifying whether distraction has been a factor.[6]

Texting While Driving

The American Automobile Association (AAA) Foundation for Traffic Safety cites handheld phones as a major safety problem. According to a 2014 AAA study, more than 67 percent of U.S.

drivers regularly talk or text behind the wheel, despite acknowledging the associated risks.

But, as AAA Director of Traffic Safety Jake Nelson notes, "Using your phone while driving may seem safe, but it roughly quadruples your risk of being in a crash. . . . None of us is immune to the dangers of distracted driving. The best advice is to hang up and drive."[7]

Texting While Walking

Texting while walking also poses a serious safety issue. A major danger stemming from texting and walking is that pedestrians believe they have it under control. In reality, "when texting, you're not as in control with the complex actions of walking."[8] Paying attention to the phone instead of one's surroundings can be catastrophic.

The most common categories of typical pedestrian distractions include:

- Manual—physically doing something else
- Visual—seeing something that distracts you
- Cognitive—mulling over thoughts in your head

Conduct an experiment next time you are strolling with a colleague using his handheld device. (You, obviously, are walking unhindered, well adjusted, and blissful, thanks to this book.) Gently suggest that he put the device away so as not to step accidentally into oncoming traffic or bash into an innocent passerby.

Does your colleague gratefully reply, "Cheers, mate! Thanks for the helpful reminder. You just saved my life! Lunch is on me!"

Or does he mutter distractedly under his breath, "Relax. Don't worry. I'm fine. I know perfectly well what's going on around me."

When a walker gets whacked upside the head, it's always the other guy's fault. Regardless of who's to blame, the fact remains that the number of injuries involving pedestrians on their mobile phones more than tripled from 2004 to 2010.[9]

Accidents stemming from being distracted, such as texting and walking, result in a particularly high percentage of head injuries and fatalities. As a public service campaign in Washington, DC, reminds drivers, "Pedestrians don't come with airbags."

Preoccupied people fall down stairs, trip on uneven pavement, and walk into traffic.[10]

Distractions While Learning

Multitasking weakens our ability to concentrate. We are collectively losing the ability to sustain prolonged attention, and distraction results in knowledge less flexibly applied in new situations.[11] The capacity to apply knowledge from one context to another is called transference. Attempts to multitask reduce this ability.

In his book *The Shallows,* Nicholas Carr argues that the Internet has changed how we process information.[12] Although the Web enables us to find data with greater ease than when we perused periodicals at the local library branch, it hurts how we absorb and retain data. Scanning a screen has largely replaced reading a page, yielding shallow learning and poor retention.

We will delve deeper into these implications in part 2.

Working While Distracted

Repeatedly dropping and picking up a mental thread results in greater mental fatigue and more mistakes than deep immersion in a single task. When we are distracted, the brain processes and stores information ineffectively. Multitasking—constantly switching between tasks—negatively affects concentration. Task-shifting is the antithesis of concentration. Multitaskers exhibit a lower ability to concentrate and are correspondingly less efficient.[13]

Wait, there's more. Multitasking also exacts a toll in three additional areas:

- Quality of life
- Relationships
- Everything else that matters to you

No big deal.

Generational Edge?

I am frequently asked whether young people have an edge when it comes to multitasking. Does growing up in a high-tech world make one better equipped to do several things at once? It does not. As Douglas Merrill put it, "Everyone knows kids are better at multitasking. The problem? Everyone is wrong."[14]

College and high school students have the same memory limitations as adults. Regardless of age, we understand and recall less when task-shifting. Poorly acquired information results in a weak ability to transfer and apply concepts. Learning to concentrate is a life skill.

As a University of Vermont study revealed, non-course-related software applications on student's laptops are open and active more than 42 percent of the time they are engaged in schoolwork. The level of distraction among university students is epidemic.

The younger generation has a wildly inflated idea of how many things they can attend to at once.[15] Young people who attempt to perform two challenging tasks at once are deluded, because complex brain functions compete for the same part of the brain—the prefrontal cortex. It is difficult for individuals to self-evaluate how well their mental processes are operating, because the processes are unconscious.[16]

Texting, messaging, and being online while in class or doing homework has a negative effect on grade point averages because, as a Harvard study revealed, divided attention hinders our ability to encode information. The result is we remember less, or nothing at all. So-called multitasking behavior "leads to a lower capacity for cognitive processing and precludes deeper learning."[17]

She Blinded Me with Science

Efforts to multitask require the brain to switch focus extremely quickly, in less than a tenth of a second. These delays and losses of concentration add up to a poor use of time and drain our brainpower.

If we know the drawbacks of attempting to multitask, why do we keep crawling back for more?

For starters, we are pursued by a plethora of tantalizing distractions, 24/7. We can't even watch television without seeing another show advertised in a giant scroll on the bottom quarter of the screen.

Another allure of multitasking is the craving for novelty. This helps explain why we are tempted to multitask even when we know it is wrong. When stimuli signal a change to the status quo, dopamine is released. Adrenaline races through the bloodstream, regardless of whether these changes are perceived as positive or negative. This surge contributes to the attraction of new tasks over what we are currently doing.[18]

Help is on the way. The brain's executive system in the frontal lobe can assist in suppressing irrelevant information. Our executive system determines what input is extraneous and where to direct our attention.

We can achieve our goals by learning to reduce distractions. Bonus! This is an acquirable skill, one that you—Hey! I'm talking to you!—can achieve. Read on.

The Singletasking Principle

2

MYTH

Singletasking is an unobtainable luxury.

REALITY

Singletasking is a fundamental necessity.

The shortest way to do many things
is to do one thing at a time.

SAMUEL SMITH

We are not learning to singletask. We are *relearning*. Single-tasking is rooted in the dawn of humankind. Early hunter-gatherers singletasked. That's how our species survived. This book is not about introducing a newfangled way of being. It is about reclaiming our natural mental state.

▶ **Singletasking means being here, now, immersing yourself in one thing at a time.**

Multitasking means living in a state of ceaseless distraction. In case you were wondering.

Want a real-life example of singletasking in action?

Brazil's 2014 World Cup brought the U.S. team to Sao Paolo, reigniting excitement in soccer/football throughout America. The U.S. team lost a riveting 2–1 match against Belgium in overtime during the Round of 16, and the hero of the game was U.S. goalkeeper Tim Howard, whose sixteen amazing saves were broadcast over and over around the world. He was undeniably pivotal in ensuring the United States wasn't trampled, though he still magnanimously credited his teammates. The team arrived as underdogs and played what Howard described as "a world-class team with world-class players," a level of competition previously considered out of their league.

A commentator asked Howard how he maintained razor-sharp focus for a solid 120 minutes, observing, "You were almost in a trance."

Howard described how he overcame extreme pressure, including hearing tens of thousands of screaming fans: "You just zone in. You know, it's hard to explain. Once that whistle blows, everything else disappears."[1] He was singletasking.

This is how you do it. Despite the loss, Howard returned home victorious. He embodied the humble pride of a champion, acknowledging, "I don't think we could have given it more."

As Howard demonstrated, singletasking does not mean inefficiently dawdling or dully plodding along. It doesn't mean carrying one piece of paper at a time to the office shredder.

> ▶ **Singletasking is characterized by high energy and sharp focus . . . yielding exceptional results and respect.**

Singletasking requires committing to your choices. Immersing yourself.

Singletasking obliges us to address one thing at a time to the exclusion of other demands in the present moment. You can handle your next task after working on this one. This does not require completion of the initial task, just the end of the current session of time dedicated to it. Task-switching, on the other hand, makes every task take longer.

Enemies of the Here and Now

Pouting over the past and fretting about the future are relentless time thieves, robbing us of our right to singletask. All too often we are lured into the trap of thinking about what could have been if things hadn't gone awry, or worrying about a potential outcome that may never occur. Both journeys are a big waste of time, particularly if we traverse them again and again.

As a corollary, we cannot be fully productive when we are preoccupied with judging people around us. Assessing the shortcomings and flaws of others when we could be achieving our own goals is an indefensible waste of time and energy. Plus, it interferes with reaching our own potential.

The first step is awareness. Notice where your thoughts dally when you are traveling to work, starting to fall asleep, in an idle moment before a meeting, waiting in line. Does a particular thorn in your side from the past crop up? Or do you have a habitual concern about a future turn life may take? Remind yourself that mulling over the past and envisioning alarming futures is not only fruitless but also lazy—it keeps us from throwing our presence into this moment, right here. We can't change the past, predict the future, or control other people. We can only singletask in the moment to make the most positive contribution to our lives, our work, and the world swirling all around.

Think about It

Before posing a question I am prone to query, "May I ask you something, or shall I wait?" I am assessing whether that person is free to talk or is engrossed in another task. A common response is, "Go ahead, talk to me. I'm fine," while the other person trundles along with what they're doing.

At this point I generally reply, "No problem. I'll wait." Talking to someone who is simultaneously engaged in another task is a formula for failure. Many people resist acknowledging that doing two things at once is inherently detrimental, rather than proof of one's efficiency.

Recollect a recent meeting you attended. Was your mind elsewhere? The next time you attend a meeting, practice being where you are. Synchronize your mind and body. Be present.

Sometimes we don't even realize how far away our thoughts have wandered. Up next is a handy assessment designed to measure your predisposition toward being where you are.

Singletasking and You

Wondering where you land in all this?

Reflect upon your typical workweek. Using the questionnaire in table 1 on the following pages, circle the degree to which you engage in each of the following activities, using this scale:

5 = Frequently (3 or more times/week)

4 = Often (1–2 times/week)

3 = Sometimes (1–3 times/month)

2 = Occasionally (5–8 times/year)

1 = Rarely (1–4 times/year)

0 = Never

Table 1: Singletask Self-Assessment
How often do you . . .

1. Use your handheld device while driving?

3+ TIMES / WEEK	1–2 TIMES / WEEK	1–3 TIMES / MONTH	5–8 TIMES / YEAR	1–4 TIMES / YEAR	NEVER
5	4	3	2	1	0

2. Meet someone new and can't recall his or her name within moments?

3+ TIMES / WEEK	1–2 TIMES / WEEK	1–3 TIMES / MONTH	5–8 TIMES / YEAR	1–4 TIMES / YEAR	NEVER
5	4	3	2	1	0

3. Respond to a message while in a meeting?

3+ TIMES / WEEK	1–2 TIMES / WEEK	1–3 TIMES / MONTH	5–8 TIMES / YEAR	1–4 TIMES / YEAR	NEVER
5	4	3	2	1	0

4. Not know what preceded the question, "What do you think about that?"

3+ TIMES / WEEK	1–2 TIMES / WEEK	1–3 TIMES / MONTH	5–8 TIMES / YEAR	1–4 TIMES / YEAR	NEVER
5	4	3	2	1	0

5. Use your personal device while walking?

3+ TIMES / WEEK	1–2 TIMES / WEEK	1–3 TIMES / MONTH	5–8 TIMES / YEAR	1–4 TIMES / YEAR	NEVER
5	4	3	2	1	0

6. Use your smartphone while with a colleague?

3+ TIMES / WEEK	1–2 TIMES / WEEK	1–3 TIMES / MONTH	5–8 TIMES / YEAR	1–4 TIMES / YEAR	NEVER
5	4	3	2	1	0

7. Intend to do a task and instead become sidetracked?

3+ TIMES / WEEK	1–2 TIMES / WEEK	1–3 TIMES / MONTH	5–8 TIMES / YEAR	1–4 TIMES / YEAR	NEVER
5	4	3	2	1	0

8. Show up at the wrong time or place for an appointment?

3+ TIMES / WEEK	1–2 TIMES / WEEK	1–3 TIMES / MONTH	5–8 TIMES / YEAR	1–4 TIMES / YEAR	NEVER
5	4	3	2	1	0

9. Pretend you are taking notes on your laptop while engaged in another task (such as surfing the Web, checking email, or texting)?

3+ TIMES / WEEK	1–2 TIMES / WEEK	1–3 TIMES / MONTH	5–8 TIMES / YEAR	1–4 TIMES / YEAR	NEVER
5	4	3	2	1	0

10. Exit an elevator on the wrong floor because you are distracted?

3+ TIMES / WEEK	1–2 TIMES / WEEK	1–3 TIMES / MONTH	5–8 TIMES / YEAR	1–4 TIMES / YEAR	NEVER
5	4	3	2	1	0

11. Have to reread or rewatch material because you weren't focused?

3+ TIMES / WEEK	1–2 TIMES / WEEK	1–3 TIMES / MONTH	5–8 TIMES / YEAR	1–4 TIMES / YEAR	NEVER
5	4	3	2	1	0

12. Realize you aren't giving someone your complete attention?

3+ TIMES / WEEK	1–2 TIMES / WEEK	1–3 TIMES / MONTH	5–8 TIMES / YEAR	1–4 TIMES / YEAR	NEVER
5	4	3	2	1	0

13. Keep your personal device on the table at meals and check it regularly?

3+ TIMES / WEEK	1–2 TIMES / WEEK	1–3 TIMES / MONTH	5–8 TIMES / YEAR	1–4 TIMES / YEAR	NEVER
5	4	3	2	1	0

14. Feel compelled to respond to work demands when "off the clock"?

3+ TIMES / WEEK	1–2 TIMES / WEEK	1–3 TIMES / MONTH	5–8 TIMES / YEAR	1–4 TIMES / YEAR	NEVER
5	4	3	2	1	0

15. Write an important note on a scrap of paper that is subsequently misplaced?

3+ TIMES / WEEK	1–2 TIMES / WEEK	1–3 TIMES / MONTH	5–8 TIMES / YEAR	1–4 TIMES / YEAR	NEVER
5	4	3	2	1	0

16. Finish workdays with the sense that you didn't get enough done?

3+ TIMES / WEEK	1–2 TIMES / WEEK	1–3 TIMES / MONTH	5–8 TIMES / YEAR	1–4 TIMES / YEAR	NEVER
5	4	3	2	1	0

17. Lose your train of thought due to media interruptions?

3+ TIMES / WEEK	1–2 TIMES / WEEK	1–3 TIMES / MONTH	5–8 TIMES / YEAR	1–4 TIMES / YEAR	NEVER
5	4	3	2	1	0

18. Hear from others that you are easily or often distracted?

3+ TIMES / WEEK	1–2 TIMES / WEEK	1–3 TIMES / MONTH	5–8 TIMES / YEAR	1–4 TIMES / YEAR	NEVER
5	4	3	2	1	0

19. Surf the Web, go on social media, or respond to messages while on the phone?

3+ TIMES / WEEK	1–2 TIMES / WEEK	1–3 TIMES / MONTH	5–8 TIMES / YEAR	1–4 TIMES / YEAR	NEVER
5	4	3	2	1	0

20. Have a lack of fulfillment and productivity, despite being busy?

3+ TIMES / WEEK	1–2 TIMES / WEEK	1–3 TIMES / MONTH	5–8 TIMES / YEAR	1–4 TIMES / YEAR	NEVER
5	4	3	2	1	0

Calculate Your Score

Now, calculate your score by adding up your total points. This score reveals your current propensity to singletask.

YOUR SCORE: _____

RESULTS

0 to 25 Points
Level 1: One Singletask Sensation

Thank you for scoring so low. Your sensational ability to singletask has, for starters, enabled me to use the heading "One Singletask Sensation," my behind-the-scenes purpose for writing this book. You are truly dedicated to living in the moment . . . or you live on a commune in a remote parcel of land without access to the twenty-first century. I hope you at least catch the news from time to time.

26 to 50 Points
Level 2: The Right Track

You will be doing a good amount of nodding while reading this book (head nodding, not nodding off). You either have a predisposition for immersing yourself in one task at a time or have consciously integrated singletasking into your life. You are on the right track, and we can get you even further along in your quest to be here, now.

51 to 75 Points
Level 3: Hope Springs Eternal

Don't stop believing. Look at the upside! There are lots of ways you can achieve a new, more effective way of working and living. Keep reading. We can beat this thing.

76 to 100 Points
Level 4: Hit the Brakes

Hey, I know some stellar executive coaches. Let me know if you'd like an introduction! No, seriously, reading this book is a fabulous step forward to making an impactful, positive change in your productivity and relationships.

The Meaning of This

The Singletask Self-Assessment enables you to determine where you land on the spectrum. Envision a line, from the most die-hard multitaskers to the most skilled singletaskers.

Multitasker ◄─────────────────────────────► Singletasker

Few people encompass entirely one style or the other. Most of us tend toward a particular side, landing somewhere along the spectrum. Stress, context, and concurrent demands can all determine how prone we are to task-switching on a given day— or during a particular week.

Sample Results

Perhaps you wonder what types of activities are most likely to ensnare us. A similar singletask self-assessment was administered to two hundred respondents representing thirty diverse professions. Table 2 presents a compilation of responses to some sample statements.

TABLE 2: Results from a Similar Singletask Survey	
HAVE YOU ENGAGED IN THE FOLLOWING BEHAVIORS ONCE OR MORE PER WEEK?	**AFFIRMATIVE RESPONSES**
Sat at the computer to do something and got sidetracked into doing something else?	91%
Heard a name and couldn't remember it a moment later?	91%
Used your personal device while walking in public or in high-traffic areas?	87%
Been with a colleague and responded to a text or instant message from someone else?	52%
Responded to an instant message while on a call or in a meeting?	50%
Realized during a meeting that you did not remember what was last said?	49%

The top three questions have astoundingly high positive response rates. The remaining questions have affirmative responses for about half the respondents. Task-switching is enticing indeed. And the impact of being so distracted damages careers, communication, and credibility.

Progress?

The Industrial Revolution (circa 1760–1840) marked a seismic shift in the technological age. The telegraph and telephone became widespread in Western Europe and North America, beginning a societal trajectory that marked the end of the world as we knew it. Suddenly, people could be beckoned at any time. Technology stormed our lives, luring us away from the people and events directly in front of us. Singletasking became increasingly difficult to maintain.

Carl Jung (1875–1961), the founder of analytical psychology, described his visit to Africa in 1925: "My companions and I had the good fortune to taste the world of Africa. . . . Our camp life proved to be one of the loveliest interludes in my life. I enjoyed the 'divine peace' of a still primeval country. . . . Thousands of miles lay between me and Europe, mother of all demons. The demons could not reach me here—there were no telegrams, no telephone calls, no letters, no visitors. My liberated psychic forces poured blissfully back to the primeval expanses."[2]

Jung referenced the "divine peace" of fleeing the technological "demons" of early twentieth-century Europe. He cherished escaping telegrams and phone calls. Now, a mere ninety years later, we can hardly imagine considering such basic technological devices any real threat to our privacy or peace of mind.

What are your modern-day versions of "technological demons"?

Start a list, whatever comes to mind. You can include devices, social media platforms, or any version of technology. Spending two or three minutes of your time on the list sounds about right.

Our minds cannot keep up with the speed of technology. Despite the promises of devices to make our lives easier and simpler, we live with increasing peril of social isolation and of threatened privacy and security.

Encounters

Martin Buber (1878–1965), a philosopher and a contemporary of Jung's, examined the impact of high- and low-quality interpersonal relationships. He shares how cultures free from modern distractions have a connectivity reflected by their language: "In the beginning is relation. Consider the speech of 'primitive' peoples . . . whose life is built up within a narrow circle of acts highly charged with presentness. The nuclei of this speech . . . indicate the wholeness of a relation. Zulu have a word for 'far away' which means . . . 'There where someone cries out: O mother, I am lost.'"[3]

Buber cited people's increasingly pervasive sense of alienation in the early twentieth century. He attributed this to the underlying meaninglessness of an ever-growing percentage of interpersonal encounters. He professed that life is about the creation of meaningful interactions and identified two primary modes of relating to others, translated from the original German as "thou" and "it."

My Technological Demons

_____

_____

_____

_____

_____

_____

_____

_____

_____

_____

_____

_____

_____

_____

_____

_____

_____

The *thou* approach understands life as a series of encounters. We engage others as active participants in a shared dialogue. *Thou* interactions are concrete and authentic. Buber believed that every interaction—however brief or transient—has infinite potential.

The *it* style treats others as objects to analyze and use. Discussion boils down, more or less, to a series of monologues. In this mode, we don't truly "meet" people; instead, we assess how they can be of service. Buber considered this mode of interaction a lack of real encounters, devaluing life and the meaning of existence. He lamented the uptick of the *it* interactive style: man is alienated, life is meaningless, because we no longer value the *thou* mode of encounter. Many modern ills come from this dehumanization.

The cost of disengaged encounters is high, according to Buber, because true living depends on meaningful interactions with depth. As he said, "All actual life is encounter."[4]

Today we engage ever more heavily in *it* interactions. Mentally absent from those physically present, we half listen while conversing electronically with people physically absent.

▶ **The practice of singletasking returns us to being where we are, restoring whole relationships and real interactions.**

Welcome, my friend, to the crisp and cheery world of singletasking.

Pull up a chair. We are going to have a little chat about your relationship to your brain. After all, you take it nearly everywhere you go.

PART TWO

Regain Control

Concentrate all your thoughts
upon the work at hand.
The sun's rays do not burn until
brought to a focus.

ALEXANDER GRAHAM BELL

3 Your Mind

Multitasking demonstrates competence.

*Singletasking demonstrates
discipline and focus.*

Focus and simplicity. You have to
work hard to get your thinking clean,
to make it simple. It is worth it because
then you can move mountains.

STEVE JOBS

As noted, singletasking means taking control of your environment and your mind. Singletasking is not only what you do in the world; it is also about developing willpower.

If you meet someone and instantly forget his name, there's a solid chance your brain wasn't present when he said "Hector" because you were preoccupied with other matters entirely. The inability to concentrate on another person when being introduced or holding a conversation is evidence of an undisciplined cerebellum. What I call the *Scattered Brain Syndrome* (SBS) is at least partially attributable to the fact that we are hesitant to be alone with our thoughts.

Do you consciously manage your thoughts, perceptions, and reactions? Or do you squander your brain waves thinking about how much better life would be if external factors changed? Do you allow a zillion thoughts to zing through your head simultaneously? Or do you choose how to direct your attention as you glide gracefully through your day?

Practicing singletasking means taking back the reins and setting your own agenda.

The temptation to multitask is heightened when we feel beholden to the perceived demands or presumed expectations of others, rather than to our own priorities. This is often linked to an anxiety-inducing desire to be valued.

Much has been written, including here, about the challenges of external stimuli. Devices can be alluring, seducing us to ditch the Singletasking Principle. We will explore how to manage those distractions. Yet we must also address our internal response to the media, smartphones, and tablets.

Assume responsibility for how you process stimuli. For many, the ever-expanding multimedia environment is just the latest excuse to avoid looking within. It is all too easy to replace inward examination with external distractions. As popular comedian Louis C. K. observed, "People are willing to risk taking a life and ruining their own because they don't want to be alone for a second, because it's so hard."[1]

Are you addressing or avoiding real-life challenges? How much time each week do you allocate for personal development, compared to the time you spend online? Beyond controlling your devices, control your mind.

It's not so easy to get right. Start in bite-sized morsels.

Many people find it very challenging to simply think. Creating a structure for your reflection time can make it easier. I journal for ten to fifteen minutes a day because writing helps me assess what I'm thinking. For some, taking a walk clears the head. Others say devoting just a few minutes to meditation makes the entire day go more smoothly. Work with your natural preferences. Consider what you enjoy and see whether you can implement a mindfulness practice. Even five minutes a day is worthwhile.

Another approach to focusing your mind is simply this:

▶ **Decide what matters most to you in a given situation, and commit.**

Chapter 7 ("Home Sweet Home") expands on additional ways to refresh your mind, enabling clearer thinking and stronger singletasking.

Shrinkage

Your reward for reading this deeply into the book (it's a brief book; don't let it go to your head) is to learn an astonishing scientific finding about the brain. It also happens to be one of the most compelling reasons I've come across for mellowing the heck out.

▶ **Overloading yourself with too many competing stimuli**
   shrinks the brain.

The prefrontal cortex shrinks from the stress of constant overload. The amygdala takes over, flooding the brain with negative emotions such as fear, aggression, and anxiety. As gray matter shrinks, we become cognitively impaired.[2] Doing too much results, quite literally, in being unable to think clearly. Extreme busyness is associated with decreased brain tissue in areas responsible for regulation of thoughts and feelings.

MRIs reveal images of the brain struggling between competing tasks.[3] The brain is overwhelmed by dueling demands. Attempting to multitask releases cortisol, the "stress hormone," diminishing the ability to process information. Stress associated with trying to multitask shrinks brain neurons, reduces problem solving, and decreases emotional regulation, resilience, and impulse control.[4]

My advice to you? Don't sweat it.

Immersion

Immersing oneself in an experience means designating full attention to the task at hand. When fully engaged in a task you enter a flow state, a concept highlighted in *Flow: The Psychology of Optimal Experience.*[5] Deep task absorption results in a state of flow—being engrossed in an activity to the point where one achieves a higher than usual level of competence.

Precisely when total immersion is likely to occur depends on your personal style and interests. Flow can arise from engaging in the visual arts, athletics, music, dance, cooking, reading, hiking, crafts and hobbies, volunteer work, or mental challenges such as gaming. Your own flow experiences may even include, say, stamp collecting (if you don't have much going on in your life).

▶ **Task-switching wipes out the possibility of a flow experience.**

Multitasking personifies a *monkey mind.* The concept of monkey mind originated in Buddhism and refers to an unsettled, restless, inconsistent, confused, or uncontrolled mind. Such a state is the antithesis of flow or immersion. Flow requires a state of singletasking.

Absorption in a task increases creativity and confidence, resulting in superior outcomes. Task immersion evokes:

- Energy and well-being
- Positivity and good humor
- Contentment and fulfillment

Simultaneously, task immersion dissipates:

- Stress and pressure
- Self-doubt and anxiety
- Boredom and distraction

Singletasking is concomitant with immersion. A colleague of mine stays on track by imagining someone he admires is sitting right next to him, observing his level of achievement. The upcoming pages are filled with additional methods to increase your ability to singletask and to work in a heightened flow state.

Parking Lot

Singletasking does not require discarding thoughts that are not aligned with your current endeavor. Instead, adopt a practice that enables you to place unrelated insights aside until the time comes to redirect your mind.

Perhaps you are familiar with the concept of a "parking lot" in meetings. Too many of us have been foiled by sloppy meetings with topics that veer all over the place. Perhaps a meeting has been designated to discuss a new reporting structure, which leads someone to bring up the need for biannual performance reviews. Her point might be valid, yet it lacks direct relevance. A few more tenuously related subjects are mentioned and you become collectively gridlocked in a snarl of topics.

The clock ticks ominously overhead.

Enter the parking lot, a flip chart or whiteboard upon which the meeting facilitator makes a list of raised topics that are best set aside for a more appropriate time. A visible list makes capturing parking lot items clear and overt.

You can adapt this technique when working independently, to focus on your current task without allowing your own thoughts to become sidetracked. When embarking on a task, keep handy a designated place to notate items for your own parking lot. You can create a Notes page on your smartphone or use a notebook. I do not recommend Post-its®, the back of receipts, or envelopes from discarded junk mail. I learned this the hard way.

When an idea strikes that is unrelated to your current task, don't let it distract you from what you've begun. Write it down and go back to what you are doing.

Why not just hope you'll remember it later? Because:

▶ **If it's on your mind, your mind isn't clear.**

Pausing to write down an ancillary thought does not lessen your commitment to singletasking. Let's say you are working in a room with natural light, in the late afternoon, and the sun begins to set. The room darkens. Do you hunker down, thinking, "I won't turn on the light, as I am intent on my work," or do you briefly stand to flip the light switch and return to your task, better equipped to work without squinting? Just as it is nonsensical to sit in the dark, failing to modify your surroundings to enable smooth progress, taking an idea out of your head and onto a page is at times necessary to maintain full concentration.

If I have an unexpected revelation, I want to capture it immediately. I get it out of my head and onto paper—to work through, expand, or toss out later. If I don't write down an insight for future reference, I either forget it or I try to keep it at the forefront of my mind—a distraction from my primary task.

Scribing a word or two clears the mind, reducing distraction. Many people tell me they have terrible memories, using that as an excuse for losing ideas, not following up on obligations, missing deadlines, and forgetting promised deliverables. Most of us have faulty memories to some degree. The quality of your memory is irrelevant! What matters is having a system in place to manage your thought processes.

Separation

We live in a world of devices that combine many functions. The smartphone, a modern-day Swiss Army knife, brandishes a plethora of features. Who would have imagined, twenty years ago, that a phone could include a camera, an alarm clock, a map, and a flashlight—for starters. Replacing several devices with just one is a widely regarded benefit of smartphones. Is there a downside?

Consider this. A challenging day draws to a close; you are ready for sleep. The last action you take before closing your eyes is setting your alarm clock for the next morning. Picking up your phone to use the alarm clock feature, you notice that three messages have unexpectedly accumulated—inducing sleeplessness. Every sleep expert in the known universe admonishes us to create a peaceful, quiet, calm atmosphere before bedtime to encourage a graceful slide into sleep. Remember when reading a nice book eased you peacefully into slumber? An unruly mobile device is the antisoother.

I used to turn off my alarm clock by, well, turning off my alarm clock. Then I switched over to using the alarm on my smartphone. Less to pack on business trips! Yet my day starts with an onslaught of tweets, texts, and messages. And if I glance at the time in the middle of the night and accidentally spy a stressful post? Forget about returning to a blissful dream state.

I had started putting my grocery list in the Notes section of my phone. It's easy to update and always with me. The drawback? When shopping I was also on the receiving end of client calls, emails, and Instagram. Plus, I was prone to walking the aisles with my head down, squinting at a small screen.

I am grateful to computers. Editing is infinitely easier than in pre–word processor days. On the flip side, now the Internet is a tantalizing keystroke away. I'm reminded of a *New Yorker* cartoon of a guy looking at a pop-up box on his computer screen that reads, "The Internet wants to destroy your productivity," with a single option to click: "Always allow."[6]

I enforce a policy of silenced mobile devices during my presentations. If a message must be returned, I ask people to take it outside so no calling or texting takes place in our shared space. In most cases, participants just put their phones away. It is really amazing to be in a program with sometimes hundreds of people who are all concentrating on the people and discussions taking place right in front of them.

Meanwhile, I always integrate participant-based activities into my presentations, and these are sometimes timed. It is simple to use the timer on my phone. Conflict of interest! Using the timer on my phone has the unintended side effect of reconnecting me with everything on my phone, most of it unrelated to the session.

Happily, this is all easily resolved. I sought out an old-school stopwatch that I wear around my neck on a cord. It's pretty cool.

How about going back to using a real alarm clock? There are plenty of spiffy designs and svelte travel versions.

Write your shopping list on paper or print out the electronic version before hitting the store.

When doing detailed work on your computer, consider going off-line to really concentrate on a document.

Our minds are easily led off track. Unbundling functions helps.

If Your Phone's So Smart, Can You Teach It to Heel?

A colleague heard about my work on singletasking and reflected on the struggle some people have keeping their electronic devices under control. He decided this is analogous to training a puppy. Puppies are appreciated for their appeal and frenetic energy. They are a bundle of potential. So, too, are smartphones!

Why do some [dogs or electronics; fill in the blank] grow into well-behaved, loveable members of the family and others become a hindrance to a sane existence, spreading chaos wherever they tread?

We both know the answers: Training. Tough love. Discipline.

It is high time to teach your smartphone how to heel, sit, and get off the nice new carpet. It's not your dog's fault. It's not your phone's fault. It's your thumbs doing the tapping.

In fact, while we're skirting around the matter, you may as well get accustomed to the idea that it is always your responsibility to take control of situations. Blaming the media (however pesky), your work (however daunting), or other people (however tedious) is the definition of futile. Look it up. Really. No, don't.

Fences

Ignoring the onslaught of distractions in our lives seems to require superhuman strength. I don't have it—do you? Place a steaming hot plate of cheese fries in front of me and I'll eat every last one. Still, if I go through my day without any cheese fries mystically emerging, I'm just fine without them.

The further removed we are from temptation, the better positioned we are to stick with our best intentions. Technology isn't the problem. The way you handle it in your life is the crux of the matter.

Let's say you're sitting at your desk, on a client call. You lean back in your chair, facing your desktop. An instant message darts across your screen. Some colleagues are picking up lunch down the street; do you want anything? Not wanting to miss the opportunity for a personal delivery from your favorite Thai dive, you quickly type back a lunch order. At that moment you hear the client ask, "Do you agree with that strategy?" Unfortunately, you have no recollection of the statement that preceded her question.

There are endless variations on the above situation. It is exceedingly difficult to not reply in the moment—a few seconds of your time and you are set with an unexpectedly delicious meal. Yet the price turns out to be quite a bit higher than the cost of lunch. I can nearly guarantee that your client noticed the slight pause between her question and your response. And your request that she repeat what she just said did not exactly enhance her opinion of your competence.

I am not suggesting that you stoically resist the urge to reply to incoming messages. It is really quite hard to ignore distractions. So let's nip this in the bud. We can create "fences" to prevent potential distractions from reaching us when we're occupied elsewhere.

When I need to concentrate on a meeting, phone call, project, or any critical task, I mitigate distractions before they happen. I prepare my work space. All ringers, chimes, and pings are muted. In fact, I keep these muted the majority of the time. I also turn off visual alerts and social media messaging. If you prefer to leave these alerts on, then turn away, cover up, or turn off your screens during meetings or scheduled calls. No peeking. On top of this, I tidy up my desk—a mess is also a distraction.

I am fortunate to have a windowed office with a decent view, so I sometimes turn myself away from my desk to face the window for the duration of a phone call. This technique tends to backfire during an in-person meeting, however.

Let's say you want to singletask but don't have much time to devote to a phone call. Easy. Simply let the caller know up front: "I'm glad we've touched base. I have fifteen minutes to discuss the plan for tomorrow's meeting." Give a gentle reminder when you have five. Then provide complete single-mindedness during this brief conversation. Some of us erroneously believe that because we aren't visible to someone else we can get away with sneaking in little extras during a call. Release this misconception to achieve stronger outcomes and save time in the long run.

It is infinitely superior to be fully present on a brief call than partially present on a long one. In the process, you are demonstrating respect for the other person's time.

Similar techniques can be employed when singletasking on your computer. Though covering your screen is not an option in this circumstance, you can still turn off auditory and visual alerts. Keep open window tabs to a minimum. Notify colleagues that you are temporarily unreachable. Resist the urge to make or receive phone calls during the time designated for this project.

Finally, get to know your devices. Learn what internal functions or apps exist to assist you in your dedication to a single-tasked lifestyle. Do you have a Favorites or Groups feature? This allows you to screen for only family messages, for instance. The Do Not Disturb option is also standard on most devices and is quite useful. Also consider options to disallow pop-up messages on your home screen, if they prove a greater hindrance than help.

This is just to get you jump-started.

You're going to beat this thing! Aren't you so excited?

4 Your Days

MYTH

Singletasking is unproductive.

REALITY

Singletasking is the most productive way to get things done.

There's never enough time to do it right,
but there's always enough time
to do it over.

JACK BERGMAN

There is an outside possibility that you feel overwhelmed because you can't seem to get everything done. How do some people manage to get so much accomplished in a day?

The *Harvard Business Review* reported on the work habits of highly effective employees.[1] Besides getting immediately to work upon arrival, these employees also took regular breaks throughout the day. Integrating recharge time into their daily schedule made them more efficient overall. High performers even singletask during lunch—they don't do work while enjoying their midday meal.

Take note! We accomplish more by allowing pockets of rest time. Engrossing ourselves in tasks when we're "on" is the other side of the coin. Even so, how do you survive a day with too many demands?

A Day in Your Life

Perhaps you are plagued by unhelpful thoughts such as, "I can't do it! Ackkk! Save me from drowning in my own to-do list!"

Help has arrived. I spoke with a diverse range of professionals about the types of activities they may hope to complete in a single morning. I compiled a list, removed the specifics for broad application, and put together two ways to tackle this list over the course of a workday morning.

Meet Dave.

Here's what Dave says he *needs* to do one morning:

- Proofread and send a proposal to a client
- Attend an internal staff meeting

- Give a performance review to a direct report
- Participate in a conference call
- Get on the chief information officer's schedule
- Respond to or delete 200+ emails
- Present recommendations to the transition committee

Also, his wife is giving a big presentation to her main client this morning, and he promised to meet her for lunch near the office at 12:15 p.m.

Take One: An Ever-Expanding Mess

Dave arrives at work and heads to the lunchroom to grab some coffee. Lisa and Ted are there, pulling him into a fifteen-minute conversation about the previous evening's networking event. They have a few laughs, and he tells himself it is a good way to start the day and build rapport. Plus, he doesn't want to be rude.

He gets to his office and notices a note on his chair from the new accounting manager, placed there after Dave left work yesterday. Dave needs to fill out data input forms to be included in the upgraded payroll system. Reluctantly, he heads downstairs to take care of it. After all, better now than never.

Back up at his office, his junior staffer, Nelson, is waiting, sitting in the guest chair, armed with a pile of papers. Nelson launches into a diatribe about the incompetent marketing team, dramatically waving a flyer in the air as evidence. Dave half listens while he searches for emails he can mindlessly delete. He wants to be a supportive supervisor, yet he needs to balance that with getting some of his own work done for a change.

Just then, Betty cheerily pops her head in his door to remind him that the staff meeting is about to start. Everyone is assembled down the hall except Dave. He sputters an expletive, grabs his tablet, and follows Betty out the door. At least he got away from Nelson.

Dave abhors staff meetings, so he makes the most of his time by pretending to take notes while actually instant messaging with Ted, seated across the table from him. He also shoots off a couple of emails in response to the hundreds that are continually piling up. At one point Grace, his boss, asks for Dave's input, but he has no idea what topic is being discussed. He plays it off, saying he's getting old and his hearing must be going. Finally, the meeting ends.

The day is escaping him. He shoots off a text to his direct report Karissa, saying that he must, again, postpone her annual performance review. He glances over the big proposal due at noon. The conference call begins, but he continues to scan the proposal—he doesn't have a choice. He hits Send, later realizing that a few dates were inaccurate. He makes a note to shoot off a follow-up email in the afternoon, rectifying the errors, and tosses it atop his perilously looming to-do pile.

He runs upstairs to check with the chief information officer's executive assistant about whether he can meet this week. He figures it is best done in person. She is busy with a scheduled meeting, so he waits. Suddenly he realizes he missed the window to provide recommendations to the transition committee. He is fifteen minutes late for lunch with his wife, and irritated by his morning.

Take Two: Singletasking Saves the Day

Dave knows he has a packed morning ahead, so he arrives twenty minutes early, grabs a quick coffee from the still-quiet staff kitchen, goes into his office, puts a Post-it note on his shut door that says ***Under deadline, please refrain from knocking,*** and spends five minutes organizing his morning's tasks. He filters out those that are unnecessary. He highlights those that are crucial.

Next, Dave looks for ways to carve out time for key tasks. For instance, he sends a message to Grace explaining that he has mission-critical deadlines this morning and asking if he can just attend the first half of the routine staff meeting. He promises he will be fully present during the time he attends. Dave then quickly emails his recommendations to the transition committee.

He spends the next half hour quietly and carefully proofing his client proposal. He turns off all auditory and visual alerts. He sends the proposal off with confidence and opens his office door.

Dave has scheduled the performance review with his direct report Karissa early, before things get too hectic. When Karissa arrives, Dave joins her on the visitor's side of his desk—both to build rapport and to separate himself from electronic distractions. Dave tells Karissa the appraisal will only last fifteen minutes, during which time he will give Karissa his full attention. He promises no interruptions.

Suddenly, Nelson descends on the office like a tropical hurricane, ranting about the incompetence of the marketing team. Dave interrupts Nelson's harangue, pointing out that he is in the middle of a meeting and can't engage with Nelson at the moment. Dave tells Nelson, in a friendly yet firm tone, to schedule a meeting, and immediately returns to Karissa's performance review.

Dave stops by the internal staff meeting, afterwards settling into fifteen minutes of responding to, organizing, and deleting emails. He delegates several task requests, forwarding the content to others on his team. He can't believe how many emails are moved out of his in-box when he is truly focused.

Dave has a few minutes before the conference call, so he phones the chief information officer's assistant to see if he can schedule a meeting for later in the week. She is busy, and promises to email him later with options for times.

Although he is no fan of conference calls, Dave commits to actively participating. Difficult as it is, he resists the urge to respond to emails and messages while on the call. He can discern when others are not engaged and admittedly finds it unprofessional. When the topic proceeds beyond his realm of contribution, he removes himself from the call. Dave heads out with enough time to pick up flowers for his wife en route to their lunch.

Debrief

Jot down some of the techniques Dave employs in the second version of his morning that might be particularly useful for you. For example, dedicating a mere three to five minutes at the start of each workday to organizing your to-do list can transform your entire day into one that is proactive rather than reactive.

Strategies for a Saner Workday

_____

_____

_____

_____

_____

_____

_____

_____

_____

_____

_____

_____

_____

_____

What strategies can you employ in your quest for saner workdays? For example, many of us break into a cold sweat when even contemplating the idea of delegation (read: relinquishing full control). However, delegating is important not only to free up your time but also to professionally develop those who work with you. Also, asking others when they actually need to receive something can save you much strain related to cramming in tasks before they are required.

Your Turn

List what you do for three days. Select three upcoming, more or less typical workdays. Decide upon a handy method to note your actual use of time over this period. Smartphone, notepad, stone tablet and chisel—the choice is all yours.

As you stumble through your day, write down the primary tasks you engaged in throughout. You can scribe from the beginning of your workday. You don't need to break the day into tiny segments or provide loads of detail. You just want a reality check of where the heck your time goes.

Here's an example. (If you don't want to be unduly influenced, skip ahead!)

DAY ONE

8:30–9:30	Arrived at office, greeted colleagues, made coffee, reviewed emails
9:30–10:30	Phone call regarding upcoming industry conference
10:30–11:30	Reviewed notes from meeting, surfed the Web
11:30–12:30	Lunch with coworker, complained about low office morale
12:30–2:30	Department team meeting, total waste of time
2:30–3:15	Met with information technology expert to fix computer virus
3:15–3:30	Hung out in coffee room
3:30–3:45	Phoned school counselor regarding kid's poor grades
3:45–4:00	Stared out the window, wondering how to motivate my kids
4:00–5:00	Responded to most urgent emails
5:00–5:30	Left voicemails for people I hoped were gone for the day

Obviously this is purely fictitious, created solely from my imagination. Now do your own on the next three pages.

What techniques worked for you?

Where did you stumble?

What advice would you give a peer wanting to be more productive?

What do you want to do differently tomorrow?

Day One

_____
_____
_____
_____
_____
_____
_____
_____
_____
_____
_____
_____
_____
_____
_____

Day Two

_____

_____

_____

_____

_____

_____

_____

_____

_____

_____

_____

_____

_____

_____

_____

_____

Day Three

_____
_____
_____
_____
_____
_____
_____
_____
_____
_____
_____
_____
_____
_____
_____

Also keep in mind this helpful, if irksome, rule of thumb: If there is a pressing, daunting task you are tempted to avoid, do it as early in the day as possible. Bite the bullet! Tough love, baby. Putting off a crucial task can weigh heavily on your mind, making singletasking on everything else much more difficult.

Clustertasking

What are related groups of tasks that you might do several times during an average workday? A few of my own examples include reading and responding to messages, taking items (articles, papers to sign, letters to mail) to other offices in my building, returning phone calls, and scheduling interviews.

To use this clustertasking technique, identify similar tasks. Group them together into a few combined segments during the day rather than allowing the same types of activities to constantly interrupt your train of thought.

Clustertasking saves time. Some tips for success:

- Clustertask during the times of day you're most alert.
- Do like tasks in clusters one to three times a day.
- Decide how long you will clustertask and set an alarm to remind you when to stop.
- Avoid engaging in these tasks outside of the designated time.

Are you perilously distracted by texts and emails throughout the day? Does social media lure you away from bigger tasks, to the detriment of impending projects? If so, perhaps you will decide to try clustertasking. Begin by confining messaging to three twenty-minute segments during the day: upon arrival, preceding lunch, and before heading out.

You are skeptical. Don't people have the expectation that messages will be returned more expediently? I am not suggesting that you reply to emails once a week. Three times a day is reasonable.

In addition, many email strings are unnecessarily lengthy because of the frequency of back-and-forth communication. Conversation chains can be eliminated or cut shorter by saying, for example:

- No need to reply.
- Thanks, signing off for the day.
- Only respond if there is a change.
- [Colleague] can handle it, no need to cc me.
- Great. See you then.
- I'm off-line for the next couple of hours.
- Contact [Colleague] for arrangements.

Doing this prevents future emergencies. Even on days when I have an intense deadline, for instance, I always start my day with designated time to review my schedule and plow through messages that have accumulated since the day before.

Let's say you have been out of the office for a few days and return to a landslide of demands in the form of messages, papers, and blinking lights. Don't panic. I have a system for this very situation. I call it $1 \times 10 \times 1$, and it's a variation on clustertasking.

Do an initial sweep of your awaiting demands and immediately handle any that can be addressed in one minute or less.

This might include a quick email reply, signing off on a project, returning a voice mail, or answering a scheduling request. Next, handle tasks that can be completed in less than ten minutes. Address this group as early in the day as possible. The remaining requests are those that take up to an hour of your time. Integrate these into your schedule over the next few days.

It is best to whiz through as much as possible in the morning, before the office fills with activity.

Post-it

The humble Post-it note is your first line of defense. Whether you're at the helm of an office with a working door, in a cubicle, or at a desk in a mod open floor plan, Post-its are your friends. Write your intention on a Post-it and place on the door, at the entry, or on the edge of your desk.

Observe a couple of sample Post-its my clients made to alert others that they are occupied. Humor and lightheartedness helps. Artistic ability is purely optional.

This does not make you off-limits indefinitely. The longest time frame to be unavailable maxes out at about ninety minutes. It is best to limit the length of your intensive singletasking sessions anyway, stopping before you burn out. You will be more productive and more enthusiastic about the task.

You can helpfully write the end time on your Post-it, such as **Please return after 1:30 p.m.!**

All interruptions are not created equal. There's a difference between being unavailable to shoot the breeze and not helping out during a time of real need.

I am against the acclaimed open-door policy, which presupposes interruptions are welcome and expected. For the uninitiated, an open-door policy means that your (real or metaphorical) door is open to unplanned visitors constantly. You are magically available at all times to all people. In reality, this is impossible. Being available to everyone all the time means being present for no one, ever. After all, if I'm in your office and Ray cruises in for a convo, how are you truly available for either of us? You aren't, and thus you waste everyone's time.

Make a sign-up sheet on your online calendar or at your office entry point, stating your office hours. Yes, people really do this. And it works.

Your Schedule

When you create a work schedule for your weekly obligations, include at least two open half-hour blocks of time each day to clustertask and to be available for unexpected events. I call this *flextime.* It requires discipline, but I've seen this system in place for even the busiest senior executives. A schedule of back-to-back meetings sets you up to fall hopelessly behind. You can also use open times to singletask toward completion of long-term projects. Consider "unscheduled" blocks to be real appointments that can't be double-booked unless something urgent pops up. That is part of the purpose of building flextime into the day.

Adopt the approach of a family practice doctor's office. If you want an appointment for a nonurgent basic annual exam, you may be told the next appointment is a month from today. However, if you call at 8:00 a.m. with a fever and dizziness, they offer an appointment that morning. This is because internists leave openings in their schedules for emergencies.

For a busy professional, this is an ideal model. You don't need to drop everything for a chatty coworker. Yet, if your schedule is blocked solid, you won't be available for unanticipated calamities that are bound to arise.

What about loiterers—people who cruise by your office randomly and regularly with no clear agenda or intention to depart? Or let's say you are housed in an open office, without any borders at all?

I've got you covered. Singletasking does not rely on a dream backdrop. A loiterer deposits himself at your doorstep. He is bubbling over with information about his latest fantasy football draft pick. You are under deadline. You respond by:

- Glancing up, noting that you're swamped, and looking back down
- Smiling and pointing at headphones, used to deter unwanted conversation

- Responding, "That's cool. I've got a lot on my plate," and returning to your work

The reality is that the list of what you can do or say to stave off wanderers is endless. You just need to do it. A pleasant expression and a warm smile while delivering the news that you are not available to engage in small talk goes far.

Some folks in an open office plan lament that singletasking is impossible. After all, distractions abound and boundaries are absent. Do not despair. Committed singletaskers have a stronger ability to block out distractions than those who regularly task-switch.[2]

Singletasking requires dedication and personal accountability. We cannot require an idyllic environment in order to single-task. We cannot place ourselves at the whim of people and events swirling around us. If there is a lot of conversation around you, invest in a white noise machine. They cost next to nothing and last for years. And when you achieve a flow state, external distractions don't penetrate.[3]

What about those days when you're just not able to channel your highest powers of concentration? Most open offices include a few quiet rooms. Use them if needed.

Putting systems in place mitigates interruptions while letting people know your momentary retreat is purposeful and temporary. People appreciate information about your schedule, and as an extra advantage, you will receive fewer nonurgent messages.

Demonstrate attentiveness by being conscientious about letting people know when they can expect to hear back—and make sure you follow through. Remember to restore your voice mail and email autoresponses to your regular outgoing messages. This is far more effective and respectful than attempting to be available when you're really not.

Practice, Practice, Practice

Singletasking is a learned habit. Select one way to enhance your ability to singletask. Pick something concrete, such as managing unscheduled visitors, turning off social media, designating time to plan each day, remaining focused in meetings, or clustertasking emails. Note each day that you demonstrate your desired behavior (table 3). Success four days a week is a victory. Reward yourself after fifteen workdays—beyond the inherent reward of improving your ability to be in the present moment.

TABLE 3: Noting Days of Desired Behavior				
MONDAY	TUESDAY	WEDNESDAY	THURSDAY	FRIDAY
1	2	3	4	5
6	7	8	9	10
11	12	13	14	15

Many of the examples provided are standard workplace scenarios. However the concepts are transferable to any context in which you have many responsibilities, whether you are a freelancer, a student, an artist, or a stay-at-home parent.

Your Interactions **5**

Singletasking means letting people down.

Singletasking means giving others your full attention.

Every action done in company
ought to be done with some sign of respect
to those that are present.

GEORGE WASHINGTON

I've been asked, "Isn't singletasking ultimately a selfish act? Doesn't singletasking mean accepting that I'll be letting people down?"

No . . . and no. Singletasking is not self-serving, dismissive, or rude. It's for others, and it's for you. Singletasking means setting a good example. Plus, you're much more present for others.

I was invited to facilitate a New Leader Training session to build rapport between Liz, a newly appointed senior executive, and her recently inherited team of thirty employees. Liz reached out to me because she recognized the value in strengthening communication within work groups. She was willing to invest the time and resources required for a full-day, off-site training session to achieve her goal of building a strong working relationship with her department.

We began the program promptly at 9:00 a.m. Liz was forty-five minutes late. She arrived breathless, explaining she was dealing with a last-minute crisis at the office. That was the beginning of the end. Over the course of the program, she was outside the room more than half the time. Arguably, eight hours is a long day. Equally arguably, it is not.

My "new leader" was proud of her ability to multitask. Liz was accomplishing (aka checking off her list) a team-building program to ingratiate her to the team while simultaneously taking care of issues back at the office. In reality, she could have more successfully handled the office issues upon her return. Nothing was life-or-death. I wasn't dealing with a brain surgeon stepping out of the operating room to work on a team problem-solving puzzle. I can say that Liz wasted a lot of time and resources on a training that provided the opposite of what she intended—the assurance that she was sincerely invested in her team.

Unfortunately, the impact of the program was lost. Sure, the participants bonded and learned a lot of useful communication skills, yet the most frequent comment on the follow-up evaluations was: Why wasn't the team leader participating? Liz's diffused attention only reinforced the perception that she didn't really care. That was what the team learned from the experience.

Like most senior executives, Liz is a very busy person. Being busy doesn't impress upon a team that you care. Being present—mentally and physically—does.

Liz told her team that they were her priority, yet her actions belied her words. After the session, a participant emailed me a pertinent quote by Lewis Cass: "People may doubt what you say, but they will always believe what you do."

The adage holds true: actions do speak louder than words. This can also work in your favor. Team and leadership development is an investment with dividends that can even exceed technical training. A leadership study conducted by psychologist Daniel Goleman found that interpersonal competency is twice as important as intellect (IQ) and technical expertise as an indicator for superior managerial performance.[1]

A few months after the "Liz Incident," I did similar training for a different organization. Again, the senior executive, Ricardo, was late. However, he phoned in advance and explained the reason, which happened to be a valid work-related emergency. Ricardo arrived about twenty minutes after the start time, apologized, and hit the ground running. He was fully engaged the entire off-site, despite compelling reasons to be in touch with the office.

Ricardo also directly acknowledged and addressed his personal challenges, such as a propensity to lose his cool in meetings, explaining that he was working on it and that it stemmed from his desire for the organization to excel. People do not expect perfection; they just really value honest, open dialogue. When the evaluations were turned in, the number one "best part of the training" cited was Ricardo's involvement and openness. The program renewed hope in an organization that previously had been facing a major divide between senior executives and midlevel managers.

Singletasking leaders demonstrate a commitment to their work and their teams. Regardless of the proclaimed reason, trying to multitask can convey arrogance, disrespect, disorganization, and disinterest.

Lasting Inspiration

A client of mine, Samuel, recounted to me his encounter with Henry Kissinger thirty years prior. Kissinger had flown into Sam's town to speak at a conference. His luggage was lost, and he needed a shirt. Sam, a young man at the time, was volunteering at the event. He ran out to buy Kissinger a shirt. As Sam described it,

> When I returned, Kissinger gratefully accepted the shirt
> that I had selected for him. He maintained eye contact,
> and all of his attention was directed solely at me during

the encounter. I'll never forget his considerable ability to make contact with me at what seemed to be the exclusion of all else. He made me feel as though I was the only other person in the universe. A brief encounter, to be sure, yet the impact lasted a lifetime. It's an understatement to say Kissinger is a great man, with many responsibilities. He certainly didn't need to worry about me. But he did. And I'm certain this skill must have served him well as a world diplomat.

At the time of this notable encounter, my client was in no position of power or influence. Nonetheless, during their brief engagement, Kissinger's complete focus was on him. Sam still recalls Kissinger's gratitude and respect as clearly as if the interaction occurred yesterday.

Kissinger provided a plum example of how even an extraordinarily busy person can give his full attention to the person right in front of him.

Listen to Me!

Listening isn't just about hearing words. It is about demonstrating respect and building rapport. Real listening requires energy and commitment.

When I conduct 360-degree feedback assessments, one of the most shocking and common results for executives is that they are perceived as untrustworthy. This does not mean they are unethical. It usually indicates the leaders don't prioritize their staffs' needs.

Failing to give others our full attention is highly correlated with multitasking. And focusing on someone for a few minutes is far more productive than conducting an hour-long "coaching" session while simultaneously doing several other tasks.

A conversation I recently had with a client about his new supervisor went like this:

"He respects me."

"How do you know?"

"He listens to me. And he knows I appreciate him because I pay attention to what he is saying."

When demonstrating the value of active listening in a seminar, I typically do a two-part role-play with hapless participants. In the first, I behave like—let's face it—a typical self-important manager. As my role-playing employee speaks to me about a challenge he is facing, I multitask. I tidy up my office, whip off a reply to an instant message, prep for a client presentation, and halfheartedly respond to his inquiries. As the "conversation"— and I use that term loosely—wraps up, I assure him he is welcome to stop by any time. Stepping out of role (I am normally an astute and sensitive listener, no doubt!), I ask the participant who took the role of my employee two questions:

1. Did you feel listened to?

2. Would you come speak with me again about a future problem?

The answers to both are consistently no.

Here's the rub: I somehow coerce the now wounded participant into a do-over. He reenters with the identical fictional problem. This time I sit down to listen, inviting him to pull up a chair as well. I make eye contact, reflect back what he says, and give him my full attention.

Another difference in the second round is that this time I begin the conversation by informing him that I only have a few minutes to talk, as I must shortly begin preparations for an important client meeting. I solve none of his problems. Instead, I ask him what he has done toward resolving the issue and what he suggests as plausible next steps for resolution.

Upon conclusion of the second round, I ask the class which scenario took longer. Regardless of the topic—and it is different each time, as determined by the participant—the second scene always takes less time.

In the debrief, I ask the volunteer whether he felt put off when I began the conversation by pointing out I could only give him a few minutes of my time. No one has ever minded. People are not insulted that we are not at their beck and call. Receiving undivided attention for five minutes seems universally preferable to being held hostage in someone else's hectic office for forty-five minutes, while scores of other tasks take precedence over the meeting itself.

A major reason people give for not really listening is that they don't have the time.

▶ **We don't have the time to *not* listen.**

A major benefit of actually listening is noticing how much is communicated beyond the spoken words. Immersed in the conversation, you'll start picking up on the ceaseless cues people send out about what they really think, what they care about, what makes them excited or nervous, and so forth. You'll notice subtle nonverbals, shifts in tone, changes in body language, increases in volume, and what causes a smile or a nervous glance.

Focusing on the person in front of you is almost like obtaining X-ray vision! You will be able to see past the patter and look much deeper into what really matters to others—what they really intend to communicate—far past what's verbalized. With increasing frequency you will begin to hear, "You really understand me." Being engrossed in a conversation with a directed mind has enormous benefits. You can improve workplace relationships, win contracts, get promotions, and learn a whole lot about what makes people tick.

R-E-S-P-E-C-T

Think of times when someone you admired demonstrated respect for you or for others. What signals that someone respects you? Write down a list of up to ten examples.

Here are some sample responses collected from my clients.

1. Make eye contact.

2. Ask for and use my name.

3. Make sure I'm comfortable—be warm; put me at ease.

Ways To Show Respect

_____

_____

_____

_____

_____

_____

_____

_____

_____

_____

_____

_____

_____

_____

_____

_____

4. Offer a firm handshake.

5. Ask my opinion and demonstrate an interest.

6. Don't talk down to me—make it clear we both have useful things to contribute.

7. Thank me; express gratitude for a job well done.

8. Learn and remember facts about me.

9. Acknowledge and share my accomplishments.

10. Be pleased to see me.

What are the commonalities between your list and the one above?

Sincerely and consistently demonstrating these behaviors indicates that one is engaged in singletasking.

Some people fret that they're somehow being rude by single-tasking. Two common concerns include:

1. I need to turn things off and isolate myself to concentrate. Any interruptions break the flow, making it frustrating to get back into a complex task.

2. I multitask because people will consider me disrespectful if I don't respond immediately.

Singletasking is a matter not only of changing your own habits but also of changing others' expectations. I think that's the tricky part.

If you have a need for solitude to complete a task, honor that need as well as you can. Some people thrive on interruptions while they work, finding that energizing. Others prefer privacy to do their best work. If your work style is to minimize interruptions, then you owe it to yourself and your job to do so.

You do not need to give instant responses to every query. That is impossible, and the path to burnout. Manage others' expectations by letting them know you've received the request and when you will respond. When you do respond, give the matter your complete attention. The bottom line is delivering quality. Shakespeare was really on a roll when he observed, "All's well that ends well."

Plugged In Means Zoned Out

Technology helps us in myriad ways. However, the culture of being constantly plugged in can backfire big-time. In the workplace, being sidetracked by social media reduces productivity, harms relationships, wastes time, and lowers the ability to filter out irrelevant data. Highly successful, high-income professionals are more likely to perceive texting, emailing, and being online in meetings as unprofessional and an annoyance. Researchers at the University of Southern California's Marshall School of Business found that:

- 86 percent of executives say it's inappropriate to take phone calls during formal meetings.
- 84 percent of executives believe it's rude to write texts or emails during formal meetings.
- 75 percent of executives find it disrespectful to read texts or emails during meetings.
- 66 percent of professionals think it's inappropriate to go online during meetings.

Senior professionals equated being constantly plugged in with the following personal traits:

- Lack of respect—treating those outside the meeting as more important than those present
- Lack of attention—incapable of focusing on one item at a time
- Lack of listening—failing to demonstrate evidence of truly hearing others
- Lack of power—being unable to resist the demands of others[2]

Meetings are a petri dish for observing the spread of the electronic virus. Consider a staff meeting. What did you see twenty years ago? A long table surrounded by chairs inhabited by participants. What was in front of them? I'll go out on a limb here and say paper and pens, presumably to take notes. Perhaps to jot questions. At worst, to doodle. And now? Tablets, phones, laptops, notebooks (electronic, naturally), and increasingly elaborate handheld devices—all importantly flipped open and on, ostensibly to take electronic notes.

We are not fooled. Take a surreptitious peek at the person sitting next to you. I'd bet you a dollar he is messaging, surfing the Internet, playing an online game, Facebooking, or what have you. More often than not, plugged in means zoned out of the discussion at hand.

Even worse, consider the dreaded conference call. You have the call on speaker; both hands are free. You have the ability to mute at will. You are free to schmooze with a colleague cruising by your desk, peruse email, visit LinkedIn, check out Instagram, send a few tweets, text, check scores, wish a happy birthday to someone you're not entirely sure you know . . . you catch my drift. You're making good use of your time! Or are you?

After succumbing to one of those temptations, have you ever had zero clue about the current topic of discussion? Or have you been asked your opinion when you weren't listening at all?

Maybe you think you hid your task-switching. The rest of the crew is none the wiser. Or are they?

Think about a recent incident when you were on a call and could clearly perceive that the person you spoke to wasn't really listening. Perhaps there were barely perceptible little pauses between your inquiries and her responses.

Partial attention shows. And managers report frustration due to time wasted rebriefing others about topics already discussed at meetings that everyone attended.

Favor Who's Present

Lunching with a coworker and your phone keeps vibrating? Meeting with an employee and an important email pops up? Taking a walk with family and texts pour in?

How can you singletask when you are assaulted with urgent, clashing demands?

Give precedence to the person in person.

I recently walked into a café where I was the only customer placing an order. I already knew what I wanted and was about to make my request when the phone next to the cashier rang. He picked it up and asked, "May I help you?"

It turns out that aliens exist, and the caller was placing an order to feed an entire planet's worth of them. I haplessly shifted my weight from one foot to the other as again and again the cashier inquired, "Anything else?" propelling the caller into another litany of demands. I was hungry, in a hurry, and tired of standing in an invisible queue.

If you are in a service profession (and honestly, who isn't?), put the in-person customer first. She showed up at your establishment. Show gratitude. The phone caller can be asked to "Hold, please." Giving a phone caller precedence is a big pet peeve of consumers.

Lights, Camera, Action

Perhaps you agree with the concept of singletasking but are unclear how to stand your ground in an actual exchange. Behold the gems ahead.

TALKS WITH YOUR BOSS
Scenario 1
You are booked solid and your boss approaches you with an urgent, time-intensive demand.

> **BAD**
>
> **Boss:** I need the results of our renewed alternative status reconfiguration by three o'clock at the latest!
>
> **You:** Today?

Boss: I have a conference call to present my findings at 3:15.

You: I am in a peer-mentoring meeting until 11:30 and am presenting for a brown-bag lunch on motivation from 11:45 to 2:00. I could work on it, I suppose, from two to three, although my annual performance appraisals for my five direct reports are due at five o'clock today.

Boss: Um, what? I was just tweeted by one of our d**n investors. I've only got a couple minutes for you. So, we're good?

You: Ah, okay, yeah.

GOOD

Boss: I need the results of our renewed alternative status reconfiguration by three o'clock at the latest!

You: I'm completely booked with hard deadlines today.

Boss: *What?* I have a conference call at 3:15 to present my findings! This is mission critical!

You: Agreed. I could join the call at 3:20 to bring the team up to speed on our progress to date. Is that helpful?

Boss: Ah, sure, I guess. I've got an investor on the phone; can you shoot some bullets to me?

You: I'm facilitating that peer-mentoring program you initiated; the next session starts in a few minutes. It's going great, by the way.

Boss: Really? Our board was asking about that yesterday evening.

You: We can discuss the results early next week. How's Tuesday morning?

Boss: Sure. Does 8:30 work?

Scenario 2

You are finalizing a $1.5 million project proposal, due tomorrow. It is an initiative that is expected to make or break agency morale.

BAD

Boss: *[Via email or instant message]* We are under a serious deadline for the new team-driven supervision initiative! I need to talk to you immediately!

You: *[Pushing your proposal to the side]* Okay, what's up?

GOOD

Boss: *[Via email or instant message]* We are under a serious deadline for the new team-driven supervision initiative! I need to talk to you immediately!

You: *[Via auto-reply]* "I am currently under deadline for a major federal initiative. Please leave your contact information and I will get back to you by tomorrow morning."

Boss: *[Via phone]* Pick up! Where the hell are you?

You: Hi. I'm working on that Request for Proposal you assigned me. It's due tomorrow morning. I'm making good progress. What's up?

Boss: What proposal? Never mind. I need you to high-tail it to my office for a brainstorming session for this blasted supervision initiative. Can you get here in five?

You: I can't. I'm on the finishing touches that will cinch our chances to be selected for the organization's cutting-edge professional development program. You made me promise I'd make it my top priority. You'll love the final product. Can I forward it to you later this afternoon?

Boss: Huh? Yeah, that'd be great.

You: Super. I'm turning off my audio alerts until I've completed the finishing touches.

Perhaps you are wondering what to do if your boss says, "Too bad. You're still helping me." How do you respond?

Be specific. Say, for example, "So you want me to head over to your office in the next few minutes? To be clear, that means I will not be presenting at the brown-bag lunch as planned— how would you like that covered?"

Elements for Success
- Show respect for your supervisor and yourself
- Clarify what is agreed to and what will occur
- Share how you've exceeded expectations to date
- Offer to meet in a timely fashion

ARGUMENT WITH COWORKER
Scenario
Coworker enters your office to get responses to messages he sent regarding tomorrow's presentation.

BAD

Coworker: Hello, anyone alive in there? I've shot over three IMs in the past hour! I've got to get back to this client ASAP. Why are you ignoring me?

You: Ever heard of knocking? I'm working. You should try it sometime. *[Speaking into the phone]* You won't believe where we ended up hanging out last weekend!

Coworker: What's your problem? You're a huge bottle-neck. I'm appeasing the client and you're in la-la land. Respond to my messages; is that asking too much? You make me look bad.

You: Check the mirror; your looks have nothing to do with me. I need to work overtime to fix all your typos. Your writing is terrible. Wait, hold on a minute. *[Typing response to instant message]*

Coworker: Forget it. I'll answer the client without your input. *[Storming off]*

GOOD

Coworker: Hello, anyone alive in there? I've sent you three IM's in the past hour! I've got to get back to this client ASAP. Why are you ignoring me?

You: I'm not ignoring you, just finalizing our submission for tomorrow's industry presentation.

Coworker: That's nice, but our client needs a final sign-off on his new ad campaign. Could you spare two seconds?

You: I just want to make sure our ten minutes in the spotlight is well spent. I think you'll really like the results. I can definitely give you more than two seconds if I can wrap this up first.

Coworker: Nice, but you've ignored my three messages.

You: Sorry, I meant to put on an autoresponse. With an uninterrupted hour I can get this thing done and then really support the work you've been investing in the client. How's two o'clock in the small conference room?

Coworker: Okay, that'll work if we really knuckle down.

You: Agreed! You'll get my full attention.

Coworker: Cool. See you at two o'clock. *[Returning to his office]*

REFLECTIONS

As the apology in the "good" scenario indicates, ideally you will prearrange fences (see chapter 3). Also, expect that your coworker may be skeptical ("Okay, I guess"). However, if you prove that your word is good by demonstrating complete focus when you are working with him, he will experience the benefits and begin to accept your parameters. You can singletask several items in one day.

What if you are enveloped in a work culture that embraces so-called multitasking? One professional posed the following dilemma: "I interviewed someone for a senior job today and he listed 'ability to multitask' as a strength on his CV. The assessment tool we used for him likewise presented multitasking as a benefit. What is the best way to respond to tools like these, such as job descriptions, procedure guidelines, etc., that encourage or require multitasking?"

First, recognize that many multitasking references are not accurate uses of the term. Dig a little deeper into the intended meaning behind the usage. For example, one job description requiring "the ability to multitask" went on to explain the actual requirements: "the same person must serve in-person and phone customers." That really just means the candidate must have the capability to provide both face-to-face and remote customer service. This is not the same thing as demanding she speak simultaneously to customers on the phone and to those standing in front of her.

Similarly, when someone proudly lists a top asset as his ability to multitask, ask for an example of this trait. When I do this, I frequently hear about strengths such as staying calm under pressure, handling a number of different tasks over the course of the day, and being flexible. These are all admirable skills and not related to doing competing tasks at the same time. Trying to do so, as we've seen, reduces overall effectiveness.

No Is the New Yes

Repeat after me: "Saying no does not make me unhelpful!" It is more than okay that you can't always respond to requests immediately. How could you? Remember:

- Dropping everything for everybody is not only unrealistic, it is a formula for chaos.
- People want you to be responsive and reliable; single-tasking is the ticket.
- Attentiveness to the current task demonstrates responsibility.
- You can create autoresponses stating major deadlines and when you will return messages.

"No, I can't right now" is not equivalent to "No, I won't ever do it." What you are really conveying is that, just as you are committed to your current obligation, you will be equally committed to the next item on your docket—rather than continually pushing half-finished items aside.

Few of us have life-or-death jobs . . . and those who do have systems in place to manage true emergencies. Contrary to how things appear in the moment, the world will not spin out of orbit if you do not take every call immediately.

Be the Change

One of the biggest concerns I hear about singletasking is the fear that it will damage relationships. In reality, being continually online and constantly available does far more to damage your professional credibility.

Perhaps others around you want immediate responses to their demands. Who wouldn't? I'd like a steaming hot latte, pronto! That is not the point. You want to position yourself as a solid, dedicated, innovative professional. Which path will get you there faster—clear boundaries and focus or partial attention and distraction?

Attempting to be all things to all people does not prove your dedication. Instead, this diffusion of attention gives the impression that you are spacey and inconsistent. Singletasking allows you to regain control of your interactions.

PART THREE

Recall What Matters

To be everywhere is to be nowhere.

SENECA

Action ≠ Results

6

MYTH

I'm too busy to singletask.

REALITY

*I'm too busy **not** to singletask.*

Never confuse action
with activity.

BENJAMIN FRANKLIN

"I am so busy."

"Yeah? Well, I am soo busy."

"You wish. I am sooo much busier than that."

There's a busyness epidemic spreading like crabgrass taking over a lawn. Yet the hustle and bustle of activity and the presumed reward are not linked. Keeping busy does not necessarily mean you are working effectively. Leslie Williams, president of LeaderShift Consulting, astutely observed, "Our culture is in a trance about how we define productivity. We seem to measure our effectiveness by how many tasks we're doing at once."[1]

Too many people fill their lives with action disproportionate to tangible results; relatively few activities are valuable enough to deserve the allocated time. As a result, we are distracted and discontented, living lives of increasing professional pressure.

Our reigning cultural script links doing more with mattering more. Our sense of importance seems bizarrely tied to wearing ourselves out. As Laura Vanderkam pointed out, there is a strong correlation between being busy and feeling important: "By lamenting our overwork and sleep deprivation . . . we show that we are dedicated."[2]

We seem to have forgotten a few basics. For example, managing our time differently can greatly enhance our lifestyle. Joseph Juran captured this concept in *Juran's Quality Handbook*, with the Law of the Vital Few. He and coauthor Joseph De Feo explain that a key to high-quality work is to distinguish between the "trivial many" and the "vital few." He recommends scanning your tasks for what is essential and putting aside the rest.[3] Once your primary work is complete you can assess whether the rest qualifies for your attention or never did in the first place.

What deserves status as the "vital few"? Priorities are not always immediately apparent. What matters most may initially appear superfluous. Take, for instance, how little U.S. senators value spending a bit of downtime with their colleagues across the aisle.

The Most Important Meal of the Day?

The present-day Congress may be the least productive in history. Ashley Parker points out that a generation ago Republican and Democratic senators regularly dined together in the Senate dining room, "a scene almost unimaginable in today's polarized climate." The Senate dining room is now largely vacant, and the "reasons for the dining-room decline are reflective of the causes of the general polarization of Congress." Parker quotes Senator Sheldon Whitehouse: "Considering how pressed we are for time, locking in a whole lunch is a lot."[4]

Today's senators are too busy to chat over a meal with colleagues. Getting to know each other seems to be a dismally low priority. Meanwhile, rapport is low, contention runs high, and little gets accomplished. Sharing a bite across partisan lines may turn out to be the best use of a half hour in a senator's week. This is another example of how singletasking can pay off. Dedicating a brief period of time to focus on each other as real people could quite possibly prevent stalemates on the Senate floor.

Where's Your Attention?

Attempting to multitask is linked to the obsession with being busy, and correspondingly, being overwhelmed. While waiting in line to board a flight near a loudly intrusive closed-circuit airport television, I overheard one traveler say to another, "We are constantly being bombarded with useless information." I agree. One lesson I learned at the University of Pennsylvania's Annenberg School for Communication was that the media can't tell you what to think, but it can tell you what to think *about*. Unfortunately, the media often tells us to think about pure dreck.

The news used to be an hour evening report on a few stations. Now we are offered news 24/7, from virtually endless media sources. Our attention spans are decreasing at the speed of light. Television commercials and music videos frequently splice together thirty images or more in a single minute. Multitasking is reflected in the media around us as segments are presented in ever-diminishing fragments. We are bombarded by distraction, as our brains become trained to avoid reflection.

Apparently, people will do nearly anything to sidestep introspection, as was shown in a University of Virginia experiment that created a stir in the worlds of psychology and neuroscience. Subjects were left alone in a room with nothing to do except push a button that delivered an electric shock to them. After six minutes, the majority of participants found it so unpleasant to be alone with their thoughts that they elected to self-administer electric shocks. The same participants previously said they would pay money to *avoid* receiving shocks.[5]

This shocking study (I couldn't resist) echoes some of our discussion in chapter 3. If you avoid time alone, consider what you are missing out on. Reflection has many benefits. According to researchers in Italy, self-awareness increases our ability to empathize: "The more in touch [I am] with my own feelings and experiences, the richer and more accurate are my guesses of what passes through another person's mind."[6]

The modern world has evolved to greatly favor doing over thinking, but we can make meaningful improvements in our lives by creating time to reflect. Convert some of that time when you're "busy" surfing the Web into a few minutes of personal reflection each day.

Dr. Ethan Kross at the University of Michigan surmises that people seek distractions to escape thinking about their lives. Contemplation is a learned skill. "If a friend comes to you with a problem it's easy to coach them through it, but if the problem is happening to us we have real difficulty, in part because we have all these egocentric biases making it hard to reason rationally. The data clearly shows that you can use language to almost trick yourself into thinking your problems are happening to someone else."[7]

One technique that may help you to integrate Dr. Kross's advice is to use third-person pronouns or your own name when writing, thinking, or speaking about challenges you face. Practicing self-reflection to work through life's challenges is one of the most beneficial applications of singletasking.

Workaholic: A Relative Term

"Make time for your personal life" is a common adage. Yet, rather than follow this sound counsel, we seem to be getting collectively worse.

Check out this 1982 description of workaholic behaviors: "You can examine your workaholic tendencies by answering the following questions: Do you take work home with you regularly? Do you accept phone calls even when trying to complete an important job or when you are taking a break? Are you reluctant to take vacations?"[8]

Consider the evolution of work expectations in the intervening three and a half decades. What was previously labeled as evidence of perilous workaholism is now the bare minimum of what most professionals practice regularly. Attending to work after hours, allowing interruptions of all sorts while addressing a pressing task, and responding to electronic messages is pervasive and expected in many professional circles. That doesn't make it right.

Some people perceive the "always available" professional as valuable and powerful. Technology makes us potentially accessible 24/7, accentuating the expectation of being continually on call, intensely busy, and eminently important. Despite advancements that presumably save time, we have somehow become busier than ever.

In 1928, John Maynard Keynes wrote "Economic Possibilities for Our Grandchildren," an essay predicting life in 2028. He predicted that the standard of living in Europe and North America would be so high by 2028 that people would work about three hours a day—and even that would be more than necessary. Keynes surmised that a major challenge facing us today would be what to do with all of our spare time.[9]

Little did he know.

Why are we so busy? What are we busy doing? As Henry David Thoreau put it, "It is not enough to be industrious; so are the ants. What are you industrious about?"

Technology designed to do things faster has largely backfired; we are perpetually short of time. Rather than freeing us from the tethers of ceaseless demands, multimedia devices at home and work fuel our overextended lifestyle. Put another way:

> If timesaving devices really saved time, there would be more time available to us now than ever before in history. But, strangely enough, we seem to have less time than even a few years ago. It's really great fun to go someplace where there are no timesaving devices because, when you do, you find you have *lots of time*. Elsewhere, you're too busy working to pay for machines to save you time so you won't have to work so hard. The main problem with this great obsession for Saving Time is very simple: you can't *save* time. You can only spend it. But you can spend it wisely or foolishly.[10]

What does it mean to save time? What is the upshot of having all these time-saving devices? It seems that even as we work so hard and purchase so much, we are still too busy to enjoy ourselves. Desperate for a solution, we try to multitask, resulting in errors, miscalculations, and dismal communication. Self-proclaimed multitaskers often have virtually no time at all. Ultimately, it is singletasking that creates breathing room.

Time-Shifting

One component of immersing yourself in a task is to build in regular breaks. Singletasking thrives when coupled with scheduled time away from the primary activity. If your work is sedentary, use your break time to move around. If you're inside, take a brisk walk outside. If your role is physically demanding, use the time to rest. Five to ten minutes is generally plenty to replenish your energy. Your own heart is a role model: "Most people have the idea that the heart is working all the time. As a matter of fact, there is a definite rest period after each contraction . . . In the aggregate, its rest periods total a full fifteen hours per day."[11]

Time-shifting means alternating periods of high productivity with time to decompress. When working on a project, take frequent breaks to keep up your energy. Scientists have proven over and over that we are much more efficient when we recharge ourselves.

In a coordinated response to digital excess, a group of organizations sponsors the National Day of Unplugging, a twenty-four-hour period without technology. That means no use of telephones, tablets, computers, radios, or televisions. This generally requires a concerted effort; many people are rarely without at least one hand-held device. Even as we sleep, a screen is inches from reach. I can hardly remember the last time I saw someone out walking a dog or pushing a baby stroller without a smartphone in hand.

Participants in the 2014 National Day of Unplugging were asked why they participated. Reponses varied from the poetic to the principled and included a desire to:

- Recharge and reboot my life

- Spend quality time with the family
- Restore the beauty of daily life
- Live in the moment
- Reconnect with the real world

You can do it.

What prevents you? Guilt for taking time off? A sense you need to be productive? A vague obligation to be reachable at all times?

Reverse those. If you must indulge in guilt, feel it when you're not mentally present. If you need to be productive, realize you'll be more productive by time-shifting. You needn't be constantly available. If it puts your mind at ease, you can let people know your intentions in advance, provide detailed outgoing messages, and perhaps, over time, change the expectation that you will be all things at all times to all people. Being always available is unrealistic. Let go of this impossible notion and free up a revived, relaxed, more present version of yourself—so when you are with someone, you are really all there. Envision the difference between a dim, fuzzed-out flashlight and a laser.

Reboot Your Life

How can you identify ways to reboot your own life? What opportunities do you have to practice unplugging for an hour or two in a typical week? Start small and think creatively.

I recommend initial steps that require little time, expense, or planning. Some examples collected from my clients include:

- Unplugged outings with friends or family
- Conversations uninterrupted by smartphones
- Hiking, walking, and enjoying nature off-line
- Writing with all electronic tones and visual pokes turned off
- Dining out with the rule that whoever plugs in pays for the meal

How about you? What would make a difference in your life? Try listing five ideas on the next page.

From here you can get more ambitious—such as taking twenty-four-hour, off-the-grid ventures.

Leisure Time Singletasked

I take a weekly step aerobics class at my neighborhood gym. It has quite the cult following; devotees will do virtually anything to attend. Why? One could cite the loveable instructor, upbeat music, or the indulgence of focusing solely on oneself for a solid hour.

Beyond this, it is impossible to participate without complete mind and body engagement. For at least one beautiful hour of the week, we participants are singletasking. The only way to keep up with the class is to immerse oneself one hundred percent—learning a new, complex routine each week that integrates movement and rhythm. The mind and body are equally engaged. We are forced to singletask, and we love it.

Ways to Unplug

As a bonus, practicing flow experiences outside of the work-place enhances the ability to streamline attention on the job. It's a transferable skill.

Slowin' Down

"Slow Reading Clubs" have cropped up around the world.[12] These clubs espouse the belief that slow is good, and science supports their claims. Reading slowly correlates with pleasure, empathy, concentration, high comprehension, and stress reduction. Clubs meet in homes, libraries, and coffee shops and follow protocol such as sitting in a quiet place, reading for at least thirty minutes without interruption, switching off phones, and disconnecting from the Internet. Reading on a tablet is allowed. Offshoots include slow cooking and slow knitting clubs. This is a fad with benefits. Intent focus on mind-stimulating activities slows the rate of memory loss.[13]

Slowing down also can be imposed on you unannounced. One caretaker of a relative with an illness that slowed his functioning observed, "My dad has slowly progressing ALS (amyotrophic lateral sclerosis, or Lou Gehrig's Disease). He can still walk, but slowly. He can still talk, but slowly. He can still cook, but very, very slowly. When I am with him I just have to find a different pace. It's hard at first, but then there is such relief that I'm not having to move so fast."

The Arts

Zentangle is the art of making patterns out of basic, deliberate strokes that build upon each other. The structured images on compact squares of paper are created in single sittings of fifteen to twenty minutes, and the art form is touted as relaxing, meditative, and enriching. Practitioners describe a pleasurable sensation as a result of their Zentangle practice. They say the increase in creativity extends to other aspects of their lives, too. As one Zentangle artist explained to me, "Zentangle is mindful, not mindless. It is relaxing, therapeutic, and puts all my other thoughts on hold." Zentangle is said to open the minds of practicing artists to unexpected thoughts and insights.

This is just one example of how artistic endeavors can relax and regenerate you during a busy day. Another lovely way to singletask in your leisure time is by heading off to the movies. Viewing a film in a real cinema, rather than at home, has many added benefits. Whereas a home is rife with distractions, watching a stellar movie in the theater is a great way to practice singletasking.

Besides being a relatively inexpensive, accessible means of entertainment, watching a great movie occupies your mind to the exclusion of whatever else is going on in your life. The storyline captures your imagination, and sitting in a comfy chair engulfed by soft darkness separates you from physical stimuli outside the sights and sounds of the movie (except, perhaps, the crunch of popcorn).

The brain processes films similarly to actual experiences. One reason some folks are drawn to adventure films is the vicarious thrill they receive. And watching a foreign or period film is a bit like taking your mind on a mini-vacation across space or time. When you are engrossed in a movie—or for that matter a book, art exhibit, or other artistic diversion—your brain is locked into the matter at hand. You are singletasking. And you emerge refreshed. It's like a deluxe shower for the brain.

The sky is the limit when identifying singletasking outlets to revive your body, mind, and spirit. Creativity extends well beyond what we traditionally call the arts. For example, many people find inspiration through volunteer activities. Stepping away from obligations and goal-driven activities to engage your whole self is the key. Creativity takes many forms; these are just a few examples.

We, as a society, are progressively busier, with ever more diffuse focus. A successful attorney wryly observed, "I don't think I know how to pay close attention anymore." Our frenetic minds result in losing touch with much of the nuance and beauty of being here, now. Take the reins; amp up your productivity by living more fully in the present.

Home Sweet Home 7

MYTH

Singletasking is for the workplace.

REALITY

Singletasking is for all aspects of life.

Always do one thing less
than you think you can do.

BERNARD MANNES BARUCH

I want you to have an inherently fulfilling, positive, rewarding, meaningful career. I just want you to be home when you're at home. Singletask it, baby.

The high-tech TiVo Roamio device can record several television shows simultaneously, enabling users to watch live or recorded shows anywhere. Isn't that wonderful?

Rather than highlighting the life-enhancing aspects of enabling consumers to never miss a show, however, a tongue-in-cheek campaign from 2014 featured users:

- Crashing into a tree from distracted downhill skiing
- Watching TiVo during a family therapy session
- Being imprisoned for watching television in the Vatican

Even the promoters of this high-tech device see the downside of splitting attention.

Home Life Quiz

Many of us aren't fully aware of the extent to which task-switching affects our personal lives. Perhaps you think you've got a handle on distractions, although others have suggested that you might reconsider your habits. Or perhaps you wonder whether you'd benefit from a change or two. If so, the Home Life Quiz (table 4) is for you. Find a cozy spot and enjoy.

Reflect on your home life. Using the following questionnaire, circle the degree to which you engage in each of the following activities, using this scale:

3 = Frequently (at least once a week)

2 = At times (at least once a month)

1 = An anomaly (rarely)

0 = Not applicable (never)

Table 4: Home Life Quiz
How often do you . . .

1. Annoy others by not fully listening when they speak to you?

1+ TIMES / WEEK	1+ TIMES / MONTH	RARELY	NEVER
3	2	1	0

2. Take your work home with you?

1+ TIMES / WEEK	1+ TIMES / MONTH	RARELY	NEVER
3	2	1	0

3. Have two or more media devices on simultaneously?

1+ TIMES / WEEK	1+ TIMES / MONTH	RARELY	NEVER
3	2	1	0

4. Go out with family or friends and spend much of the time on a personal device?

1+ TIMES / WEEK	1+ TIMES / MONTH	RARELY	NEVER
3	2	1	0

5. Replace face-to-face conversations with communication via social media?

1+ TIMES / WEEK	1+ TIMES / MONTH	RARELY	NEVER
3	2	1	0

6. Have hurried or distracted family dinners without meaningful conversation?

1+ TIMES / WEEK	1+ TIMES / MONTH	RARELY	NEVER
3	2	1	0

7. Forget about food you're preparing because you were thinking about something else?

1+ TIMES / WEEK	1+ TIMES / MONTH	RARELY	NEVER
3	2	1	0

8. Enter a room and forget why you came in?

1+ TIMES / WEEK	1+ TIMES / MONTH	RARELY	NEVER
3	2	1	0

9. Talk on the phone while on your computer?

1+ TIMES / WEEK	1+ TIMES / MONTH	RARELY	NEVER
3	2	1	0

10. Eat while walking, driving, or otherwise paying no attention to your food?

1+ TIMES / WEEK	1+ TIMES / MONTH	RARELY	NEVER
3	2	1	0

Calculate Your Score

Now, calculate your score by adding up your total points. This score reveals your current propensity to singletask in your personal life.

YOUR SCORE: _____

RESULTS

0 to 10 Points
Level 1: Très Impressive

Give yourself a pat on the back!

11 to 16 Points
Level 2: Not Bad, Not Bad

You're definitely on the right track.

17 to 23 Points
Level 3: Keep the Dream Alive

You're positioned to become more present. Stay with it.

24 to 30 Points
Level 4: Distraction Faction

Take a leap of faith and try out a few of the methods in this book. See what happens!

The extent to which you immerse yourself in one experience at a time impacts everything from your health to your relationships to your personal fulfillment. Consider the way we chew food. Multitasking during meals appears to be linked to overeating and poor digestion. Many dietary and health experts state that directing our attention to eating during meals increases satisfaction. Chewing carefully and pausing between bites reduces caloric input. Singletask eating is a weight-loss aid!

Being on social media while interacting with others gives them the not-so-subtle message that they don't matter. Also, devoting much of your personal time to idle activities reduces your sense of meaning and fulfillment. Psychologist Abraham Maslow would say it lowers your probability of becoming self-actualized (achieving your full potential).

The questions on the Home Life Quiz fall into two major categories of what prevents you from being fully present: relational and personal. Five of the questions in the survey looked at individual goal orientation and five were relational. To see what affects you most, check out table 5.

TABLE 5: Comparing Relational and Person Effects	
SURVEY QUESTION	PRIMARILY RELATIONAL OR PRIMARILY PERSONAL?
1	Relational
2	Personal
3	Personal
4	Relational
5	Relational
6	Relational
7	Personal
8	Personal
9	Relational
10	Personal

Based on your results, is task-switching more likely to harm your interpersonal relationships or pursuit of your goals?

Carving Out Time

If you are dissatisfied with your score on the Home Life Quiz, how might you rectify the situation? Where are opportunities for positive change?

Find pockets of time to connect with people who matter most to you—including yourself. Perhaps you can practice leaving your phone at the door for the first hour you are home, or designate a brief segment of each week to pursue an interest.

What about family singletasking? On car trips, are you typically plugged in separately? How can you use travel time to enrich your relationships? Family psychologists say the car is an ideal place to have meaningful conversations because eye contact is not required, making teens in particular more comfortable opening up.

There are other approaches, too. For instance, a colleague relays the following story:

> I know a family with kids who are now young adults. They are still so close. We asked them what their secret was. Their answer? A hot tub. They would take a hot tub together—or a subset of them would—every night. They would get in, relax in the warm water, not want to get out, and have no distractions. They actually talked about deep things. Better than family dinners, they decided, where people are eating, asking for the salt, and at least one person is dealing with serving or cleaning.

Although not everyone has a hot tub, the concept can be applied to numerous accessible options. Take evening or morning walks. Go on picnics. Have weekly family meetings to reconnect. Sit outside together. Roast marshmallows around a fireplace or even a candle. And if you are simply enjoying a meal together, put down your devices! I can't tell you how often I've observed families dining with each person staring at a screen rather than interacting with one another.

It is a matter of making conscious choices.

Choosing Well

There are a plethora of books with charming titles emphasizing the importance of being a perfect parent raising the perfect child. *The Good Enough Child* sets itself apart from the get-go.[1] One chapter, "The Good Enough Parent," provides a reminder about the value of making choices with a high likelihood for positive outcomes. This parenting scenario is easily transferable to virtually any context, including the workplace.

A full-time working mom has an evening ritual of reading aloud a chapter of a book to her kids before bed. One evening she is particularly exhausted and just doesn't have the energy. Still, she doesn't want to let her kids down, so she settles in to read.

She immediately becomes resentful and grumpy, snapping at her kids. She feels like a failure; her intention to be "good" results in being "bad." The author explains a fundamental, profound lesson, which basically boils down to: If you want to read, read. If you aren't up to reading, don't. Either choice is acceptable. The sole unacceptable route? Setting yourself up for failure by reading begrudgingly, despite having no energy reserves, and then short-circuiting.

There are only two decision points:

▶ **Make a choice, and then stick with it.**

You can make a different choice next time. No need to be stubborn! Simply stick with what you set out to do for the time being, rather than dissipating your energy second-guessing your decision throughout the current experience. Decide what matters most to you in a particular instance, and commit.

I made a similar proclamation earlier because I want you to get this into your head. Consider it a mantra.

Make your choice by assessing what really matters to you most. Perhaps you are feeling a bit lazy and want very much to remain supine on the sofa, catching the tail end of a *Simpsons* marathon. Still, it is your pal's birthday and you intended to stop by with her favorite treat. Replace the path of least resistance with what is more important. You will begin to notice a correlation between what matters more and what ultimately makes you feel better in the long run.

I am not implying, however, that self-sacrifice is always the way to go. Ask yourself which choice rings true for you in the moment, given the surrounding context. Your preference can change later without indicating you are the slightest bit wishy-washy or inept.

At this moment, you may want to go to sleep more than anything in the world. Unless this is a 24/7 craving, it's possibly a sound option. Momentarily choosing sleep over your job or your home life for an evening does not mean you don't value or care about your career or family. Quite the opposite. Taking care of yourself makes you a better contributor to everything and everyone else in your world.

Once you make a decision about what you are doing at the moment—or for the evening—don't second-guess or stray from your plan by sneaking in the other choice simultaneously.

Whatever you choose, do it fully. Otherwise you miss out on truly living. As Georgia O'Keeffe observed, "Nobody sees a flower, really; it is so small. We haven't time, and to see takes time—like to have a friend takes time."

This quote reminds me to be truly present where I am.

I am also inspired to make better decisions. Still, I mess up plenty, too.

A Humiliating Example of Flawed Logic

As Ms. Singletasker herself, I still catch myself foolishly attempting to task-switch from time to time. I tell my family and friends to call me out if they catch me "cheating." Even with steadfast conviction, changing behaviors requires vigilance.

There are myriad excuses for "one little exception"—I'm lost; traffic made me late for an appointment; it's to do a good deed; I really can handle it; etc.

It doesn't get any better (or, rather, worse) than this: While working on *Singletasking*, I convinced myself that it was perfectly reasonable to attend yoga class while concurrently editing my book. I would sneak in a few pages of my manuscript, folded to the relevant section, and cached close to my mat. This haphazard arrangement lasted a few days, until I took a particularly demanding class. It was impossible to turn the pages while managing a solid downward dog. Forced to focus solely on my practice, I reaped the benefits of a better workout, returning to my work revitalized and more productive.

As any two-bit practitioner knows, a real yogi devotes her body and mind to an hour-long class. Not to mention that the manuscript in question, as you are well aware, touts the virtues of singletasking. Combining tasks really does add up to less than the sum of the parts. I never brought my manuscript to yoga again.

What is often called living in the moment can also be described as singletasking your way through life.

A Happy Perk

Singletasking is the gift that never stops giving. In fact, according to Dr. David Goldman, a key to happiness is being immersed in the moment.[2]

Pay attention, ladies and gents, to that idea. Singletasking is correlated to happiness. This is big. Why do you think it's the case?

Scientists explain that people are more fulfilled when fully engaged. Beyond the golden elixir of effectiveness, we are happier when singletasking.

In 2010, Harvard University engaged 2,250 adults to assess mood and involvement levels at random intervals. Happiness turned out to be directly correlated with high task engagement. As a corollary, the study also found that easily distracted people were less likely to be happy.[3]

Psychologist Viktor Frankl would have had something to add to this conversation. Much of his life's work was devoted to discerning what makes some people fulfilled, regardless of circumstances. He identified a strong correlation between happiness and two mental processes: the ability to detect meaning in all of life's moments, and the ability to let go of the self-defeating obsession with outcome.

Today, many people with comfortable lives are so preoccupied with recording joyful events that they are at risk of missing them altogether. What is more important: cherishing every moment of a holiday, major life event, or sensory experience—or snapping a photo for subpar viewing at an indeterminate moment in the future? What is your off-the-cuff response, and do your actions support your convictions?

Let's just combine all these questions into one humdinger from an iconic 1990s rock song, "Graduate" by Third Eye Blind: "Do you live the days you go through?"

Respond to that in the affirmative, and you're stellar.

Ring My Bell

In 2007, violinist Joshua Bell, widely regarded as one of the world's finest musicians, agreed to participate in an experiment. He rode the Washington, DC, Metro to the L'Enfant Plaza station, opened his violin case on the floor for tips, and played his multimillion-dollar violin for forty-five minutes.

Few people stopped to listen. Bell earned $32 in tips. Only one demographic consistently paused to hear him play: young children. Adults were too busy to be open to this stunning, free concert by a man who can command up to $1,000 *per minute* to play.[4]

We lose our capacity for joy and wonder when we are constantly rushing. Embracing singletasking includes being open

to the possibility of unexpected moments that merit full engagement. Observing the world with partial attention as we breeze
past could mean missing a once-in-a-lifetime opportunity.

Gregory Burns discusses author Peter Kaminsky's description
of *hyperreality*. "When I am really enjoying myself," says Kaminsky,
"I call it 'special time' . . . a different reality, one in which I am
fully alive, fully focused, where each second is a ripe fruit bursting
with juice."

According to Burns, "Under the right circumstances . . .
hyperreality [creates] transcendent moments that burn in your
memory."[5]

The more practiced we become at being "fully alive," the
greater our capacity to achieve a hyperreality where we are both
happier and more capable.

Olympian Opportunities

The opening ceremony of the 2014 Winter Olympics in Sochi,
Russia, provided a prime example of how to be absent during a
peak experience.

Imagine that a lifetime of dedication and commitment
has paid off—you've earned a place on an Olympic team. The
moment has arrived; the world prepares to watch you shine
in the opening ceremonies. However, the majority of athletes
from some nations were neither soaking in the glorious moment
nor waving back to the crowds. Instead, they were gazing
into handheld devices, taking videos and selfies with which to
"remember" the event later. The desire to capture the moment

is understandable, yet certainly there would be plenty of high-quality, professional video to choose from later!

This aspect of the Sochi opening ceremonies displayed an utter lack of singlemindedness. Hundreds of athletes demonstrated how to be plugged in and disengaged. Over half of the athletes seemed to miss a peak experience.

Zen masters implore us to be here, now, even in mundane tasks such as dishwashing (a particularly tough sell for me). It is difficult to understand why so many athletes gave filming the event precedence over savoring a few miraculous moments of being the pride of their country, among the elite in the world. They missed out on the high that comes from total immersion—the singletask high.

One athlete, however, demonstrated the impact of single-tasking in the face of adversity. U.S. champion figure skater Jeremy Abbott crashed hard on his first jump during an intended quadruple toe loop in the men's short program at the Olympics.

Despite being physically injured and mentally shaken, Abbott struggled back up and finished with gusto.[6] Abbott concluded his stunning routine to a huge ovation and later commented, "I'm not the least bit ashamed. I stood up and I finished that program. I'm proud of my effort and what I did under the circumstances."

Jeremy Abbott demonstrated strength of will and character. How did he manage to complete his routine with such spirit and presence of mind? He singletasked his mind and body one hundred percent. If he had diffused his mental or physical energy by lamenting his crash into the barrier in those first seconds, he could never have pulled off the brilliant performance that followed.

The same is true for honing the skill of being here, now. The way of singletasking just takes a couple of techniques, a little practice, and the perseverance to jump back up if you occasionally skate directly into the wall.

Back to Basics

Wrapped up in the frenzy of our lives, we are prone to losing track of the basics. In this book I've made a case for singletasking. I've cited neuroscience, psychology, history, and cultural anecdotes. The most compelling evidence, though, is really from your own life.

When you short-circuit, is it from doing too much at once or one thing at a time? Think about when you feel the most creative, productive, and proud. I bet this happens when you are completely immersed in what you're doing.

Allow me to remind you of the Singletasking Principle:

▶ **Get more done, one thing at a time.**

Turns out, you have enough time after all. It's just a matter of how you choose to spend it.

Now go out there and enjoy this beautiful day . . . one sunbeam at a time.

APPENDIX
Retorts to Multitask Hardliners

Conviction is worthless
unless it is converted to conduct.

CARLYLE

How can you explain the singletasking way to those die-hard multitaskers in your life?

Enjoy this sampling of real-life statements I've collected from my loveable, delusional, multitasking friends, accompanied by snappy replies for your edification (table 6). Add your own zingers in the third column.

Go ahead and tear out this chart and carry it everywhere you go. Be my guest. Think of it as a cheat sheet of retorts.

TABLE 6: Responses to Multitaskers		
MUFFLED PROTEST OF MISGUIDED YET WELL-INTENTIONED DIE-HARD TASK-SWITCHERS	MY POLITE, YET FIRM RESPONSE, SUPPORTED BY MORE FIGURES THAN A PARISIAN FASHION SHOW	YOUR OWN DAZZLING, EDGY REPLY THAT FAR OUTPACES MINE IN SHEER BRILLIANCE
"It is 11:15 a.m. and I have two deadlines at noon. I *can't* do one at a time."	It is only humanly possible to do one thing at a time. Task-switching is the antithesis of concentration—making you less likely to meet either deadline with satisfactory results.	
"Making others wait to be accommodated is rude and selfish."	Multitasking rather than focusing on the person in front of you is rude and disrespectful of their time.	
"I am being productive by responding to emails during a boring, irrelevant, mandatory meeting."	Studies show you will be perceived, particularly by senior executives, as lacking willpower and self-control.	
"I get a hundred messages a day. I have to multitask!"	The only way to efficiently handle numerous demands is to pay attention to one at a time.	

TABLE 6: Responses to Multitaskers (continued)

MUFFLED PROTEST OF MISGUIDED YET WELL-INTENTIONED DIE-HARD TASK-SWITCHERS	MY POLITE, YET FIRM RESPONSE, SUPPORTED BY MORE FIGURES THAN A PARISIAN FASHION SHOW	YOUR OWN DAZZLING, EDGY REPLY THAT FAR OUTPACES MINE IN SHEER BRILLIANCE
"It is efficient to whip off a quick reply to an instant message while on a conference call—one less thing to do later."	This is how haphazard mistakes are made, not to mention losing credibility through trite responses to instant messages or being unable to answer a question because you weren't listening.	
"It's ridiculous to say I can't multitask. I can listen to music and exercise even harder."	The brain can process two tasks when one or both do not require your conscious thought. This does not fall under the definition of multitasking.	
"You must multitask. With all you do, it's impossible to singletask and get it all done."	I can't do more than one thing at a time and neither can you. Singletasking is the *only* way to get it all done.	
"A certain amount of multitasking is expected of us in our jobs."	Actually, being a productive, effective professional is expected of you.	
"You can't get full engagement at team meetings. Partial attention is the way of the future."	Partial attention contributes to a lack of team cohesion and an inability to achieve collective outcomes.	
"Young people can multitask well."	We are all hardwired to singletask. Age makes no difference.	
"I can multitask and still focus on everything I'm doing."	So-called multitasking makes you distracted, resulting in being partially present in your tasks and for other people.	

TABLE 6: Responses to Multitaskers (continued)

MUFFLED PROTEST OF MISGUIDED YET WELL-INTENTIONED DIE-HARD TASK-SWITCHERS	MY POLITE, YET FIRM RESPONSE, SUPPORTED BY MORE FIGURES THAN A PARISIAN FASHION SHOW	YOUR OWN DAZZLING, EDGY REPLY THAT FAR OUTPACES MINE IN SHEER BRILLIANCE
"People know multitasking can be counterproductive."	Few people recognize the negative toll of multitasking.	
"I don't want to be so intently engrossed in tasks that I'm spaced out or oblivious to the world around me."	An equivalent concern is saying, "I don't want to exercise for fear I will become too fit." That is the least of your worries, and seems like an excuse to sit around. If your highly skilled singletasking puts you at risk of, say, entirely losing track of time, set an alarm for a predetermined end time.	

And now, an all-purpose response to any general protest:

▶ **Singletasking saves time, increases efficiency, and improves relationships.**

'Nuff said.

NOTES

INTRODUCTION

1. "The Multitasking Paradox," *Harvard Business Review* 91, no. 3 (March 2013): 30–31.

CHAPTER 1: THE MULTITASKING MYTH

1. Gigi Foster and Charlene M. Kalenkoski, "Measuring the Relative Productivity of Multitasking to Sole-tasking in Household Production: New Experimental Evidence," IZA Discussion Paper no. 6763 (July 2012).

2. Linda Stone, "Beyond Simple Multi-Tasking: Continuous Partial Attention" (November 30, 2009). http://lindastone.net/2009/11/30/beyond-simple-multi-tasking-continuous-partial-attention.

3. Eyal Ophir, Clifford Nass, and Anthony D. Wagner, "Cognitive Control in Media Multitaskers," *Proceedings of the National Academy of Sciences* 106, no. 37: 15583–15587.

4. In Jon Hamilton, "Think You're Multitasking? Think Again," National Public Radio (October 20, 2008). http://www.npr.org/templates/story/story.php?storyId=95256794.

5. In Annie Murphy Paul, "The New Marshmallow Test: Resisting the Temptations of the Web," *The Hechinger Report* (May 3, 2013). http://hechingerreport.org/content/the-new-marshmallow-test-resisting-the-temptations-of-the-web_11941.

6. National Highway Traffic Safety Administration, *The Economic and Societal Impact of Motor Vehicle Crashes, 2010* (Washington, DC: National Highway Traffic Safety Administration, May 2014). DOT HS 812 013.

7. In Michael Green, "Teens Report Texting or Using Phone While Driving Significantly Less Often than Adults," *AAA NewsRoom* (December 11, 2013). http://newsroom.aaa.com/2013/12/teens-report-texting-or-using-phone-while-driving-significantly-less-often-than-adults.

8. Marcene Robinson, "Think It's Safe to Type a Quick Text While Walking? Guess Again," *University of Buffalo News Center* (February 26, 2014). http://www.buffalo.edu/news/releases/2014/02/022.html.

9. Jack L. Nasar and Derek Troyer, "Pedestrian Injuries Due to Mobile Phone Use in Public Places," *Accident Analysis & Prevention*, 57 (August 2013): 91–95.

10. Robert Glatter, "Texting While Walking? Think Twice," *Forbes* (July 31, 2012). http://www.forbes.com/sites/robertglatter/2012/07/31/texting-while-walking-think-twice.

11. Karin Foerde, Barbara J. Knowlton, and Russell A. Poldrack, "Modulation of Competing Memory Systems by Distraction," *Proceedings of the National Academy of Sciences* 103, no. 31: 11778–11783.

12. Nicholas Carr, *The Shallows: What the Internet Is Doing to Our Brains* (New York: W. W. Norton, 2010).

13. Institute for the Future and Gallup Organization, *Managing Corporate Communication in the Information Age* (Lanham, MD: Pitney Bowes, 2000).

14. Douglas Merrill, "Why Multitasking Doesn't Work," *Forbes* (August 17, 2012). http://www.forbes.com/sites/douglasmerrill/2012/08/17/why-multitasking-doesnt-work.

15. Larry D. Rosen, L. Mark Carrier, and Nancy A. Cheever, "Facebook and Texting Made Me Do It: Media-Induced Task-Switching While Studying," *Computers in Human Behavior* 29, no. 3: 948–958.

16. Paul, "The New Marshmallow Test."

17. Reynol Junco and Shelia R. Cotten, "No A 4 U: The Relationship Between Multitasking and Academic Performance," *Computers & Education* 59, no. 2: 505–514.

18. Gregory Burns, *Satisfaction: The Science of Finding True Fulfillment* (New York: Henry Holt, 2005), p. 43.

CHAPTER 2: THE SINGLETASKING PRINCIPLE

1. Tim Howard, interview by Willie Geist, *Morning Joe*, MSNBC, July 2, 2014.

2. Carl Jung, *Memories, Dreams, Reflections* (New York: Vintage Books, 1965), 264.

3. Martin Buber, *I and Thou* (New York: Scribner, 1958), 17.

4. Ibid., 10.

CHAPTER 3: YOUR MIND

1. Louis C. K., interview by Conan O'Brien, *Conan*, TBS, September 19, 2013.

2. Mark Laubach, "A Comparative Perspective on Executive and Motivational Control by the Medial Prefrontal Cortex," in *Neural*

Basis of Motivational and Cognitive Control, ed. Rogier B. Mars et al. (Cambridge, MA: MIT Press, 2011), 95–109.

3. H. A. Slagter et al., "MRI Evidence for Both Generalized and Specialized Components of Attentional Control," *Brain Research* 1177 (October 26, 2007): 90–102.

4. E. B. Ansell et al., "Cumulative Adversity and Smaller Gray Matter Volume in Medial Prefrontal, Anterior Cingulate, and Insula Regions," *Biological Psychiatry* 72, no. 1 (July 1, 2012): 57–64.

5. Mihaly Czikszentmihalyi, *Flow: The Psychology of Optimal Experience* (New York: HarperCollins, 1990).

6. Paul Noth, "The Internet Wants to Destroy Your Productivity," *The New Yorker* (September 2, 2013): 22.

CHAPTER 4: YOUR DAYS

1. "The Multitasking Paradox," *Harvard Business Review* 91, no. 3 (March 2013): 30–31.

2. Alena Maher and Courtney von Hippel, "Individual Differences in Employee Reactions to Open-Plan Offices," *Journal of Environmental Psychology* 25, no. 5, 219–229.

3. Robert M. Nideffer, "Attention Control Training," in *Handbook of Research on Sports Psychology,* eds. R. N. Singer, Milledge Murphey, and L. Keith Tennant (New York: Macmillan Publishing Company, 1993), 522–556.

CHAPTER 5: YOUR INTERACTIONS

1. Daniel Goleman, "What Makes a Leader?," *Harvard Business Review* 82, no. 1: 82–91.

2. Melvin C. Washington, Ephraim A. Okoro, and Peter W. Cardon, "Perceptions of Civility for Mobile Phone Use in Formal and Informal Meetings," *Business and Professional Communication Quarterly* 77, no. 1: 52–64.

CHAPTER 6: ACTION ≠ RESULTS

1. Leslie Williams, interview with author, Shepherdstown, West Virginia, October 7, 2014.

2. Laura Vanderkam, "Are You As Busy As You Think?," *Wall Street Journal* (February 22, 2012). http://www.wsj.com/articles/ SB10001424052970203358704577237603853394654.

3. Joseph De Feo and Joseph Juran, *Juran's Quality Handbook* (New York: McGraw-Hill, 2010).

4. Ashley Parker, "On Senate Menu, Bean Soup and a Serving of 'Hyperpartisanship,'" *New York Times* (August 20, 2014): A1.

5. Timothy D. Wilson et al., "Just Think: The Challenges of the Disengaged Mind," *Science* 345, no. 6192 (July 4, 2014): 75–77.

6. Kate Murphy, "No Time to Think," *New York Times* (July 27, 2014): SR3.

7. Ibid.

8. Michael Matteson and John Ivancevich, *Managing Job Stress and Health: The Intelligent Person's Guide* (New York: Free Press, 1982), p. 36.

9. John Maynard Keynes, "Economic Possibilities for Our Grandchildren," in *Essays in Persuasion* (New York: Norton, 1963), 358–373.

10. Benjamin Hoff, *The Tao of Pooh* (New York: Penguin, 1983), 107–108.

11. Dale Carnegie, *How to Stop Worrying and Start Living* (New York: Simon and Schuster, 1948), 129.

12. Jeanne Whalen, "Read This as Slowly as You Can," *The Wall Street Journal* (September 16, 2014): D1.

13. Robert S. Wilson et al., "Life-Span Cognitive Activity, Neuropathologic Burden, and Cognitive Aging," *Neurology* 81 no. 4 (July 23, 2013): 314–321.

CHAPTER 7: HOME SWEET HOME

1. Brad E. Sachs, *The Good Enough Child* (New York: HarperCollins, 2001).

2. In Stacey Colino, "The Reasons of Our Discontent," *Bethesda Magazine* (November–December 2013). http://www.bethesdamagazine.com/ Bethesda-Magazine/November-December-2013/Why-Arent-We-Happy/index.php?cparticle=1&siarticle=0#artanc.

3. Matthew A. Killingsworth and Daniel T. Gilbert, "A Wandering Mind Is an Unhappy Mind," *Science* 330, no. 6006 (November 12, 2010): 932.

4. Gene Weingarten, *The Fiddler in the Subway* (New York: Simon and Schuster, 2010).

5. Gregory Burns, *Satisfaction: Sensation Seeking, Novelty, and the Science of Finding True Fulfillment* (New York: Macmillan, 2006), 74.

6. Jim Caple, "After Fall, Abbot Presses On," ESPN. http://espn.go.com/ olympics/winter/2014/figureskating/story/_/id/10451479/ 2014-sochi-olympics-team-usa-fall-short-program-jeremy-abbott-presses-on.

BIBLIOGRAPHY

**I'm going to stop putting things off,
starting tomorrow.**

SAM LEVENSON

Read these books (one at a time)!

Babauta, Leo. *The Power of Less*. New York: Hyperion, 2009.

Bandler, Richard, and John Grinder. *ReFraming: Neuro-Linguistic Programming and the Transformation of Meaning*. Moab, UT: Real People Press, 1982.

Berns, Gregory. *Satisfaction*. New York: Henry Holt & Co., 2005.

Bryson, Bill. *A Short History of Nearly Everything*. New York: Broadway Books, 2004.

Buber, Martin. *I and Thou*. New York: Scribner, 1958.

Carr, Nicholas. *The Shallows*. New York: Norton, 2011.

Cashman, Kevin. *The Pause Principle*. San Francisco: Berrett-Koehler, 2012.

Czikszentmihalyi, Mihaly. *Flow: The Psychology of Optimal Experience*. New York: HarperCollins, 2008.

De Feo, Joseph, and J. M. Juran. *Juran's Quality Handbook*. New York: McGraw Hill, 2010.

Dobelli, Rolf. *The Art of Thinking Clearly*. London: Sceptre, 2013.

Ferber, Richard. *Solve Your Child's Sleep Problem*. Rev. ed. New York: Touchstone, 2006.

Fischer, Roger, and Daniel Shapiro. *Beyond Reason*. New York: Penguin, 2007.

Foster, Jack. *How to Get Ideas.* San Francisco: Berrett-Koehler, 2007.

Frankl, Victor. *Man's Search for Meaning.* New York: Perseus, 2000.

Glennie, Paul, and Nigel Thrift. *Shaping the Day: A History of Timekeeping in England and Wales.* Oxford: Oxford University Press, 2014.

Hoff, Benjamin. *The Tao of Pooh.* New York: Penguin, 1983.

Homayoun, Ana. *That Crumpled Paper Was Due Last Week: Helping Disorganized and Distracted Boys Succeed in School and Life.* New York: Perigee, 2010.

Johansen, Bob. *Leaders Make the Future: Ten New Leadership Skills for an Uncertain World.* 2nd ed. San Francisco: Berrett-Koehler, 2012.

Jung, Carl. *Memories, Dreams, Reflections.* New York: Vintage Books, 1965.

Kador, John. *Effective Apology: Mending Fences, Building Bridges, and Restoring Trust.* San Francisco: Berrett-Koehler, 2009.

Katie, Byron. *Loving What Is.* New York: Harmony Books, 2002.

Kiefer, Charles, and Malcolm Constable. *The Art of Insight: How to Have More Aha! Moments.* San Francisco: Berrett-Koehler, 2013.

Kunz, Gray, and Peter Kaminsky. *The Elements of Taste.* New York: Little, Brown and Company, 2008.

Levine, Robert. *A Geography of Time: The Temporal Misadventures of a Social Psychologist.* New York: Basic Books, 1998.

Maslow, Abraham, Bertha Maslow, and Henry Geiger. *The Farther Reaches of Human Nature.* New York: Penguin 1993.

McCrossen, Alexis. *Marking Modern Times.* Chicago: University of Chicago Press, 2013.

Oldenberg, Ray. *Celebrating the Third Place.* New York: Da Capo Press, 2002.

Pattakos, Alex. *Prisoners of Our Thoughts*. San Francisco: Berrett-Koehler, 2008.

Quenk, Naomi. *In the Grip: Understanding Type, Stress, and the Inferior Function*. Mountain View, CA: Consulting Psychologist Press, 2000.

Rechtschaffen, Stephan. *Time Shifting: Creating More Time to Enjoy Your Life*. New York: Main Street Books, 1997.

Rosenstein, Bruce. *Living in More Than One World*. San Francisco: Berrett-Koehler, 2009.

Sachs, Brad. *The Good Enough Child*. New York: HarperCollins, 2001.

Schofield, Deniece. *Confessions of an Organized Homemaker*. Cincinnati, OH: Better Way Books, 1994.

Weingarten, Gene. *The Fiddler in the Subway*. New York: Simon and Schuster, 2010.

Wolke, Robert. *What Einstein Told His Barber*. New York: Dell Trade, 2000.

Yamashita, Keith, and Sandra Spataro. *Unstuck*. New York: Portfolio, 2007.

Zack, Devora. *Managing for People Who Hate Managing*. San Francisco: Berrett-Koehler, 2012.

Zack, Devora. *Networking for People Who Hate Networking*. San Francisco: Berrett-Koehler, 2010.

Zona, Guy. *The Soul Would Have No Rainbow If the Eyes Had No Tears*. New York: Touchstone, 1994.

If you have a particular interest in a topic in this book, contact **connect@myonlyconnect.com** and receive recommendations for relevant reads from this list and beyond.

That's devotion!

ACKNOWLEDGMENTS

Keep away from people who try to
belittle your ambitions. Small people always
do that, but the really great make you feel
as if you, too, can become great.

MARK TWAIN

I SALUTE YOU

My gratitude flows to Berrett-Koehler, my family, clients, colleagues, and fellow writers full of encouragement and breakthrough ideas. I also thank those I've not met whose work and research shine insight on living a life of singletasking.

My appreciation goes out to a dandelion spray of friends who demonstrate so well that paying attention to those you value—rather than living distracted—can change the world. For fixing so many of my words, I am grateful *past* words to Katherine, John, and Evan.

Thank you to my boys for reprimanding my innocent offers to "play a game" when you knew I was supposed to be writing, for stomping out my short-lived online Scrabble addiction, for continually asking how my book is coming along, for never kvetching, for being proud of me, and for bringing me dinner when they knew I was editing. Next, we'll work on doing the dishes.

I love you far beyond Pluto (yes, it *is* a planet).

INDEX

AT YOUR SERVICE

There cannot be a crisis next week.
My schedule is already full.

HENRY KISSINGER

ONLY CONNECT CONSULTING, INC.

Clients include:

- Smithsonian
- London Business School
- Deloitte
- National Institutes of Health
- Urban Land Institute
- Cognizant
- Australian Institute of Management
- U.S. Department of Education
- Cornell University
- Transportation Services Administration
- John Deere
- U.S. Treasury
- Mensa International

PRIMARY SERVICES

- Keynotes
- Customized Seminars
- Executive Retreats
- Business Coaching
- Strategic Planning
- Business Theater
- Assessments

AREAS OF EXPERTISE

- Leadership
- Networking
- Change Management
- Team Development
- Communication
- Singletasking

OCC won the USDA Woman-Owned Business of the Year award and is a certified vendor on the General Services Administration (GSA) schedule.

Contact **connect@myonlyconnect.com** for queries on services, products, and events . . . *and* to share your singletask success stories.

ABOUT THE AUTHOR

Let the beauty you love
be what you do.

RUMI

RELEVANT STUFF
I'm author of three books and president of Only Connect Consulting, Inc. I have an MBA from Cornell University (full-tuition merit scholar) and a BA from the University of Pennsylvania (magna cum laude).

I am visiting faculty for Cornell University's Johnson Graduate School of Management, and have twice been invited on speaking tours in Australia by the Australian Institute of Management. I'm a certified practitioner of Neuro-Linguistic Programming and Myers-Briggs Type Indicator and a member of Phi Beta Kappa and Mensa.

My first two books, *Networking for People Who Hate Networking* (Berrett-Koehler 2010) and *Managing for People Who Hate Managing* (Berrett-Koehler 2012), have been translated into more than twenty languages including Cantonese, French, German, Japanese, Korean, Mandarin, Marathi, Polish, Portuguese, Romanian, Russian, and Spanish.

I've been featured in media such as ABC-TV, *British Airways*, CNBC, CNN, *Cosmo*, *Fast Company*, *Forbes*, Fox News, *Redbook*, *Self*, *USA Today*, *U.S. News and World Report*, *Wall Street Journal*, and *Women's Health*.

I'm a bit bored. Who cares about these credentials, besides my mother?

OTHER STUFF

I believe in the power of singletasking.

I believe we are increasingly bamboozled (I'm not sure by whom, precisely) to do more than one thing at a time, which is impossible.

I believe homemade cookies and a good laugh are the balm for most woes.

I love to dance. I could trip over a piece of string. I have never been able to shake my theater habit.

I take walks without my phone every day. I have three endlessly entertaining free-range cockatiels. I can't resist talking smack with dudes twice my size at the gym, insisting I can out-bench-press them. I am most alive giving presentations and tumbling haphazardly down poorly maintained waterslides.

I have benefited from applying the Singletasking Principle to all aspects of my life.

I want you to, also.

Berrett–Koehler
Publishers

Berrett-Koehler is an independent publisher dedicated to an ambitious mission: *connecting people and ideas to create a world that works for all*.

We believe that to truly create a better world, action is needed at all levels—individual, organizational, and societal. At the individual level, our publications help people align their lives with their values and with their aspirations for a better world. At the organizational level, our publications promote progressive leadership and management practices, socially responsible approaches to business, and humane and effective organizations. At the societal level, our publications advance social and economic justice, shared prosperity, sustainability, and new solutions to national and global issues.

A major theme of our publications is "Opening Up New Space." Berrett-Koehler titles challenge conventional thinking, introduce new ideas, and foster positive change. Their common quest is changing the underlying beliefs, mindsets, institutions, and structures that keep generating the same cycles of problems, no matter who our leaders are or what improvement programs we adopt.

We strive to practice what we preach—to operate our publishing company in line with the ideas in our books. At the core of our approach is stewardship, which we define as a deep sense of responsibility to administer the company for the benefit of all of our "stakeholder" groups: authors, customers, employees, investors, service providers, and the communities and environment around us.

We are grateful to the thousands of readers, authors, and other friends of the company who consider themselves to be part of the "BK Community." We hope that you, too, will join us in our mission.

A BK Life Book

This book is part of our BK Life series. BK Life books change people's lives. They help individuals improve their lives in ways that are beneficial for the families, organizations, communities, nations, and world in which they live and work. To find out more, visit **www.bk-life.com**.

Berrett–Koehler
Publishers

Connecting people and ideas
to create a world that works for all

Dear Reader,

Thank you for picking up this book and joining our worldwide community of Berrett-Koehler readers. We share ideas that bring positive change into people's lives, organizations, and society.

To welcome you, we'd like to offer you a free e-book. You can pick from among twelve of our bestselling books by entering the promotional code BKP92E here: http://www.bkconnection.com/welcome.

When you claim your free e-book, we'll also send you a copy of our e-news-letter, the *BK Communiqué*. Although you're free to unsubscribe, there are many benefits to sticking around. In every issue of our newsletter you'll find

- A free e-book
- Tips from famous authors
- Discounts on spotlight titles
- Hilarious insider publishing news
- A chance to win a prize for answering a riddle

Best of all, our readers tell us, "Your newsletter is the only one I actually read." So claim your gift today, and please stay in touch!

Sincerely,

Charlotte Ashlock
Steward of the BK Website

Questions? Comments? Contact me at bkcommunity@bkpub.com.